How to Make a North Carolina Will

HOW TO MAKE A NORTH CAROLINA WILL

with forms

Wanda M. Naylor
Mark Warda
Attorneys at Law

Naperville, IL • Clearwater, FL

Copyright © 1984, 1994, 1998 by Wanda M. Naylor and Mark Warda
Cover design © 1997 by Sourcebooks, Inc.

All rights reserved. No part of this book may be reproduced in any form or by any electronic or mechanical means including information storage and retrieval systems—except in the case of brief quotations embodied in critical articles or reviews, without permission in writing from its publisher, Sourcebooks, Inc. Purchasers of the book are granted a license to use the forms contained herein for their own personal use. No claim of copyright is made to any official government forms reproduced herein.

Second edition, 1998.

Published by: **Sourcebooks, Inc.**

Naperville Office	Clearwater Office
P.O. Box 372	P.O. Box 25
Naperville, Illinois 60566	Clearwater, Florida 33757
(630) 961-3900	(813) 587-0999
Fax: 630-961-2168	Fax: 813-586-5088

Cover Design: Andrew Sardina/Dominique Raccah, Sourcebooks, Inc.
Interior Design and Production: Andrew Sardina, Sourcebooks, Inc.

This publication is designed to provide accurate and authoritative information in regard to the subject matter covered. It is sold with the understanding that the publisher is not engaged in rendering legal, accounting, or other professional service. If legal advice or other expert assistance is required, the services of a competent professional person should be sought.

From a Declaration of Principles Jointly Adopted by a Committee of the American Bar Association and a Committee of Publishers and Associations

---

Library of Congress Cataloging-in-Publication Data
Naylor, Wanda M.
   How to make a North Carolina will : with forms / Wanda Naylor, Mark Warda.—2nd ed.
     p. cm.
   Includes index.
   ISBN 1-57071-327-8 (pbk.)
   1. Wills—North Carolina—Popular works. 2. Wills—North Carolina—Forms. I. Warda, Mark. II. Title.
KFN7544.Z9N39   1998
346.75605'4—dc21
                                                                     97-35472
                                                                          CIP

Printed and bound in the United States of America.

Paperback — 10 9 8 7 6 5 4 3 2 1

Contents

Using Self-Help Law Books...1

Introduction...3

Chapter 1: Basics of North Carolina Wills..................................5
   What Is a Will?
   How a Will Is Used
   Joint Tenancy Avoids Probate
   Joint Tenancy Overrules Your Will
   Joint Tenancy Can Be Risky
   "Tenancy in Common" Does Not Avoid Probate
   A Spouse Can Overrule a Will
   A Spouse's Share Can Be Avoided
   I/T/F Bank Accounts Are Better than Joint Tenancy
   Special Rule for Usual Dwelling Place
   Some Property May Be Exempt from Your Will
   Getting Married Automatically Changes Your Will
   Having Children Automatically Changes Your Will
   Getting Divorced Automatically Changes Your Will
   How Your Debts Are Paid
   Will Terms You Should Know

Chapter 2: Do You Need a North Carolina Will?............................19
   What a Will Can Do
   What If You Do Not Have a Will?
   Is Your Out-of-State Will Valid in North Carolina?
   Who Can Make a North Carolina Will?

Are There Different Kinds of Wills in North Carolina?
What Is a Witnessed Will?
What Is a Handwritten or Holographic Will?
What Is an Oral Will?
Should You Use an Oral Will?
What a Will Cannot Do
Who Can Make Their Own Will?
Who Should Not Make Their Own Will?

Chapter 3: How to Make a Simple Will 25
Identifying Parties in Your Will
Personal Property
Real Estate
Specific Bequests
Remainder Clause
Alternate Beneficiaries
Survivorship
Guardians
Childrens' Trust
Personal Representative
Witnesses
Self-Proving Clause
Disinheriting Someone
Funeral Arrangements
Forms
Cautions

Chapter 4: How to Execute Your Will 35

Chapter 5: After You Sign Your Will 37
Storing Your Will
Revoking Your Will
Changing Your Will

Chapter 6: How to Make a Living Will 41

Chapter 7: How to Make Anatomical Gifts 43

Appendix A: Sample Filled-in Forms 45

Appendix B: Forms 57

Index 107

USING SELF-HELP LAW BOOKS

Whenever you shop for a product or service, you are faced with various levels of quality and price. In deciding upon which product or service to buy, you make a cost/value analysis vased upon what you are willing to pay and the quality you desire.

When buying a car you decide whether you want transportation, comfort, status, or sex appeal. Accordingly, you decide among such choices as a Chevette, a Lincoln, a Rolls Royce, or a Porsche. Before making a decision, you usually weigh the merits of each option against the cost.

When you get a headache, you can take a pain reliever (such as aspirin) or go visit a medical specialist for a neurological examination. Given this choice, most people, of course, take a pain reliever needed for a headache. But in some cases, a headache may indicate a brain tumor, and failing to see a specialist right away can result in complications. Should Everyone with a headache go to a specialist? Of course not. But people treating their own illnesses must realize that they are taking a chance, based upon their cost/value analysis of the situation, that they are taking the most logical option.

The same cost/value analysis must be made in deciding to do onc's own legal work. Many legal situations are very simple, requiring a simple form and no complicated analysis. Anyone with a little intelligence and a book of instructions can handle the matter simply.

But there is always the chance that there is a complication involved which only a lawyer would notice. To simplify the law into a book like this, often several legal cases must be condensed into a single sentence or paragraph. Otherwise, the book would be several hundred pages long and too complicated for most people. However, this simplification necessarily leaves out many details and nuances which would apply to special or unusual situations. Also, there are are many ways to interpret most legal questions. Your case may come before a judge who disagrees with the analysis of our author.

Introduction

This book is intended to give North Carolina residents a basic understanding of the laws regarding wills, joint property, and other types of ownership of property as these laws affect their estate planning. It is designed to allow those with simple estates to quickly and inexpensively set up their affairs to distribute property according to their wishes.

This self-help book also includes information on appointing a guardian for minor children, thereby protecting the children from being raised by someone you would object to. In addition, you can prepare your own living will, and organ donor card.

Chapters 1 through 5 explain North Carolina law regarding wills and the passing of property at death. Chapters 6 and 7, contains information on living wills and anatomical gifts. A selection of seven sample filled-in forms is contained in appendix A. Appendix B contains the blank forms that you will use to make your will.

You can prepare your own will quickly and easily by using the forms from the book, by photocopying them, or by retyping the material on blank paper. The small amount of time it takes to do this can give you and your family the peace of mind of knowing that your affairs will be handled according to your wishes.

A surprising number of people have had their estates pass to the wrong person because of a simple lack of knowledge of what they were doing. Before using any of the forms in appendix B, you should read and understand the material in this book. As with any new topic, it is helpful to reread sections to be certain of your information. Then you should look at the sample filled-in forms in appendix A.

In each example given you might ask, "What if my spouse died first?" or "What if the children were grown?" In these and other cases, the answers given might be different. If your situation is at all complicated, you are advised to consult an attorney. In many communities wills are available at reasonable prices. No book of this type can cover every situation in every case, but a knowledge of the basics will help you to make the right decision regarding your property.

There is no worse torture than the torture of laws.
—Francis Bacon

BASICS OF NORTH CAROLINA WILLS 1

Before making your will, you should understand how a will works and what it can or cannot do. Otherwise, your plans may not be carried out and the wrong people may end up with your property. At the end of this chapter are definitions of terms you should know.

WHAT IS A WILL?

A will is simply a document in which you tell everyone who should get your property when you die. If you have minor children, it can also determine who will take care of them and manage their property. If you do not express your wishes in a will, the laws of the State of North Carolina will decide these matters.

HOW A WILL IS USED

Some people think a will avoids probate. It does not. A will is the document used in probate to determine who receives the property, and who is appointed guardian, and executor or personal representative.

AVOIDING PROBATE

If you wish to avoid probate you need to use methods other than a will, such as joint ownership, pay-on-death accounts, or living trusts. The first two of these are discussed later in this chapter. For information on living trusts you should refer to a book that focuses on trusts as used for estate planning. *Living Trusts and Simple Ways to Avoid Probate* is available from the publisher of this book.

If a person successfully avoids probate with all of his or her property then he or she may not need a will. In most cases when a husband or wife dies, no will or probate is necessary because everything is owned jointly. However, everyone should have a will in case some property, that one forgot to put into joint ownership or that was received just prior to death, does not avoid probate for some reason.

JOINT TENANCY AVOIDS PROBATE

Property that is owned in joint tenancy with right of survivorship does not pass under a will. If a will gives property to one person but it is already in a joint account with another person, the will is usually ignored and the joint owner of the account gets the property. This is because the property in the account avoids probate and passes directly to the joint owner. A will only controls property that goes through probate. There are exceptions to this rule. (If some money is put into a joint account only for convenience it might pass under the will, but if the joint owner does not give it up, it could take an expensive court battle to get it back.)

Putting property into joint tenancy does not give absolute rights to it. If the estate owes estate taxes, the recipient of joint tenancy property may have to contribute to the tax payment.

EXAMPLES
- Ted and his wife want all of their property to go to the survivor of them. They put their house, cars, bank accounts, and brokerage accounts in joint ownership. When Ted dies his wife only has to show his death certificate to get all the property transferred to her name. No probate or will is necessary.

☛ After Ted's death, his wife, Michelle puts all of the property and accounts into joint ownership with her son, Mark. Upon her death Mark needs only to present her death certificate to have everything transferred into his name. No probate or will is necessary.

JOINT TENANCY OVERRULES YOUR WILL

If all property is in joint ownership or if all property is distributed through a will, things are simple. But when some property passes by each method, a person's plans may not go right.

EXAMPLES

☛ Bill's will leaves all his property to his sister, Mary. Bill dies owning a house jointly with his wife, Joan, and a bank account jointly with his son, Don. Upon Bill's death, Joan gets the house, Don gets the bank account, and his sister, Mary, gets nothing.

☛ Betty's will leaves half her assets to Ann and half her assets to George. Betty dies owning $1,000,000 in stock jointly with George and a car in her name alone. Ann gets only a half interest in the car. George gets all the stock and a half interest in the car.

☛ John's will leaves all his property equally to his five children. Before going in the hospital he puts his oldest son, Harry, as a joint owner of his accounts. John dies and Harry gets all of his assets. The rest of the children receive nothing.

In each of these cases the property went to a person it probably shouldn't have because the decedent didn't realize that joint ownership overruled their will. In some families this might not be a problem. Harry might divide the property equally (and possibly pay a gift tax.) But in many cases Harry would just keep everything and the family would never talk to him again, or take him to court.

JOINT TENANCY CAN BE RISKY

In many cases joint property can be an ideal way to own property and avoid probate. However it does have risks. If you put your real estate in joint ownership with someone, you cannot sell it or mortgage it without that person's signature. If you put your bank account in joint ownership with someone, they can take out all of your money.

EXAMPLES

- Alice put her house in joint ownership with her son. She later married Ed and moved in with him. She wanted to sell her house and to invest the money for income. Her son refused to sign the deed because he wanted to keep the home in the family. She was in court for ten months getting her house back and the judge almost refused to do it.

- Alex put his bank accounts into joint ownership with his daughter Mary to avoid probate. Mary fell in love with Doug who was in trouble with the law. Doug talked Mary into "borrowing" $30,000 from the account for a "business deal" that went sour. Later she "borrowed" $25,000 more to pay Doug's bail bond. Alex didn't find out until it was too late that his money was gone.

"TENANCY IN COMMON" DOES NOT AVOID PROBATE

In North Carolina, there are three basic ways to own property, joint tenancy with right of survivorship, tenancy in common, and an estate by the entireties. *Joint tenancy with right of survivorship* means that if one owner of the property dies, the survivor automatically gets the decedent's share. *Tenancy in common* means when one owner dies, that owner's share of the property goes to his or her heirs or beneficiaries under the will. *An estate by the entireties* is like joint tenancy with right of survivorship, but it can only apply to a married couple.

EXAMPLES
- Tom and Marcia bought a house together and lived together for twenty years, but were never married. The deed did not specify joint tenancy. When Tom died, his bother inherited his half of the house, and it had to be sold because Marcia could not afford to buy it from him.

- Lindsay and her husband Rocky bought a house. When Rocky suddenly died, Lindsay obtained full ownership of the house by filing a death certificate at the courthouse. That was because the deed to the house stated that they were husband and wife so ownership was presumed to be tenancy by the entireties.

A SPOUSE CAN OVERRULE A WILL

Under North Carolina law a surviving spouse is entitled to a percentage of the decedent's estate no matter what the will states. This is sometimes called the *forced share*. The surviving spouse can elect to take the following amounts if the deceased spouse specifies in the will amounts less than those set out. The amount varies depending on the number of children.

- Surviving spouse with one child: Spouse receives half of the real estate; child receives the other half. Spouse receives the first $15,000 of personal property and half of the remaining balance. Child receives half of the balance after the first $15,000.

- Surviving spouse with two or more children: Spouse receives one-third of the real estate; children receive the remaining two-thirds. Spouse receives the first $15,000 of personal property and one-third of the balance. Children divide the two-thirds balance after the first $15,000.

- Surviving spouse with no children: Spouse receives half of the real estate; parents of deceased receive the other half. Spouse gets the first $25,000 of personal property and half of the balance. Parents of the decedent receive half of the balance after the first $25,000.

- Surviving spouse with no children and no parents: Spouse receives all of the real estate and personal property.

EXAMPLES

- John's will leaves all of his property (one house in his name and $27,000) to his children of a prior marriage and nothing to his wife who is already wealthy. The wife still receives one-third of the real estate and $19,000 of John's estate, and the children divide the remaining two-thirds of the real estate and $8,000.

- Mary puts half of her property in a joint account with right of survivorship with her husband and in her will she leaves all of her other property ($15,000) to her sister. When Mary dies, her husband receives all the money in the joint account and all of her other property.

A SPOUSE'S SHARE CAN BE AVOIDED

While some feel it is wrong to avoid giving a spouse the share allowed by law, there are legitimate reasons for doing so (such as where there are children from a prior marriage) and the law allows exceptions.

The best way is for your spouse to sign a written agreement either before or after the marriage. But while many spouses express the greatest fondness for their stepchildren, getting them to sign over a large share of his or her estate can be a challenge.

Another way to avoid a spouse's forced share is to have all property in joint ownership with right of survivorship with others.

EXAMPLE

- Dave owns his stocks jointly with right of survivorship with his son. He owns his bank accounts jointly with right of survivorship with his daughter. If he has no other property, his spouse gets nothing since there is no property in his estate.

Another way to leave something to someone other than your spouse and avoid the forced share is with a life insurance policy naming someone other than your spouse as beneficiary.

Avoiding a spouse's share, especially without his or her knowledge opens the possibility of a lawsuit after your death, and if your actions were not done to precise legal requirements they could be thrown out. Therefore, you should consider consulting an attorney if you plan to leave your spouse less than the share provided by law.

I/T/F Bank Accounts Are Better than Joint Ownership

One way of keeping bank accounts out of your estate and still retain control is to title them "In Trust For" or I/T/F with a named a beneficiary. Some banks may use the letters POD for "pay on death" or TOD for "transfer on death." Either way the result is the same. No one except you can get the money until your death, and on death it immediately goes directly to the person you name, without a will or probate proceeding. These are sometimes called *Totten Trusts* after the court case which declared them legal.

EXAMPLE
☛ Rich opened a bank account in the name of "Rich, I/T/F Mary." If Rich dies the money automatically goes to Mary, but prior to his death Mary has no control over the account, doesn't even have to know about it, and Rich can take Mary's name off the account at any time.

Special Rule for Usual Dwelling Place

A surviving spouse may elect to live in the homeplace for the rest of his or her life (life estate) and to own outright all the furnishings of the house. The surviving spouse can do this instead of getting what was left to him or her in the will or what his or her forced share would be, as determined earlier in this chapter.

This *usual dwelling place* provision only applies to property that is in individual ownership. Jointly held property and property in trust do not come under these rules. Property that is in the names of both spouses passes directly to the survivor outside of the will (tenants by the entirety). To avoid property becoming *usual dwelling* property, it must be purchased in joint names or in trust. If it is already in an individual's name, it cannot be put in trust or in joint ownership without the spouse's signature.

It is possible to set up the title to your home in such a way that it will not be the *usual dwelling* and your spouse cannot claim an interest in it (for example, if you want it to go to your children by a previous marriage). This should, however, be done by a lawyer who is familiar with the latest cases in this area. If it is done wrong it may be thrown out by a court. In such a situation, you should also consider a written agreement with your spouse regarding the home.

SOME PROPERTY MAY BE EXEMPT FROM YOUR WILL

If you have a spouse or minor children, then your "household furniture, furnishings, and appliances" in your "usual place of abode," and automobiles in your name can be allotted to your spouse under the *year's allowance* of $5,000. Each minor child gets a *family allowance* of up to $1,000.

EXAMPLE
☛ Donna dies with a will giving half her property to her husband and half to her grown son from a previous marriage. Donna's property consists of a $5,000 automobile, $5,000 in furniture, and $10,000 in cash. Donna's husband may be able to get the car as the $5,000 *spouse allowance*. Then he and the son would split the remaining

$15,000. (The son would get nothing if the husband also claimed a *spouse's share* as described earlier in this chapter.

Getting Married Automatically Changes Your Will

If you get married after making your will and do not rewrite it after the wedding, your spouse gets a share of your estate as if you had no will unless you have a premarital agreement, or you made a provision for your spouse in the will. See the *forced share* referred to earlier in this chapter.

Example ☛ John made out his will leaving everything to his disabled brother. When John married Joan, an heiress with plenty of money, he didn't change his will because he still wanted his brother to get his estate of $15,000. When John died, Joan got his entire estate and his brother got nothing.

Having Children Automatically Changes Your Will

If you have a child after making your will and do not rewrite it, the child gets a share of your estate as if there was no will.

Example ☛ Dave made a will leaving half of his estate to his sister and the other half to be shared by his three children. He later has another child and doesn't change his will. At his death, his fourth child would get one quarter of his estate, his sister would get three-eighths, and the other three children would each get one-eighth.

Getting Divorced Automatically Changes Your Will

If you and your spouse get a divorce, any provisions giving your spouse your assets or naming your spouse as personal representative of your estate are revoked. All other provisions of the will remain valid. If you still want your ex-spouse to receive assets or act as Personal Representative, you may do so by specifically referring to your ex-spouse in your will and stating that you are no longer married.

Examples

☞ Bonnie and Clyde were divorced after fifteen years of marriage. Clyde wanted Bonnie to get his hat collection after his death. Clyde can provide in his will that the hat collection should go to "Bonnie, my ex-wife." This clearly shows that Clyde intended his ex-spouse to specifically receive something at his death.

☞ James and Jane had also been married for fifteen years. So distraught after the divorce, James failed to change his will that left everything to "my beloved wife, Jane." Jane will not receive any property from James. Instead the property will be distributed as if James did not have a will.

How Your Debts Are Paid

One of the duties of the person administering an estate is to pay the debts of the decedent. Before an estate is distributed the legitimate debts must be ascertained and paid.

An exception is *secured debts*, these are debts that are protected by a lien against property, like a home loan or a car loan. In the case of a secured debt, the loan does not have to be paid before the property is distributed.

EXAMPLE
- John owns a $100,000 house with a $80,000 mortgage and he has $100,000 in the bank. If he leaves the house to his brother and the bank account to his sister then his brother would get the home but would owe the $80,000 mortgage.

What if your debts are more than your property? Today, unlike hundreds of years ago, people cannot inherit other peoples' debts. A person's property is used to pay their probate and funeral expenses first, and if there is not enough left to pay their other debts then the creditors are out of luck. However, if a person leaves property to people and does not have enough assets to pay his or her debts, then the property will be sold to pay the debts.

EXAMPLES
- Jeb's will leaves all of his property to his three children. At the time of his death Jeb has $30,000 in medical bills, $11,000 in credit card debt, and his only assets are his car and $5,000 in stock. The car and stock would be sold and the funeral bill and probate fees paid out of the proceeds. If any money was left it would go to the creditors and nothing would be left for the children, but the children would not have to pay the medical bills or credit card debt.

Will Terms You Should Know

The following are some basic legal terms you may encounter. Other terms are defined throughout this book.

Administrator. (Administratrix if female.) A person appointed by the court to oversee distribution of the property of someone who died (either without a will, or if the person designated as executor in a will is unable to serve). See *executor* and *personal representative*.

Beneficiary. A person who is entitled to receive property from a person who died (regardless of whether there is a will).

Bequest. Personal property left to someone in a will.

Codicil. A change or amendment to a will.

Decedent. A person who has died.

Descendent. A child, grandchild, great-grandchild, etc.

Devise. Real property left to someone in a will. A person who is entitled to a devise is called a *devisee*.

Elective share. The portion of the estate that may be taken by a surviving spouse, regardless of what is stated in a will. In North Carolina this varies from one-third to all of the estate, depending upon whether you have any children.

Executor. (Executrix, if female.) A person appointed in a will to oversee distribution of the property of someone who died with a will.

Exempt property. Property that is exempt from distribution as a normal part of an estate.

Family allowance. An amount of money set aside from an estate to support the family of the decedent for a certain period of time.

Forced share. Another term for *elective share*.

Heir. A person who will inherit from a person who died without a will.

Intestate. Without a will. A person who dies without a will is said to have "died intestate."

Intestate share. The portion of an estate that a spouse is entitled to receive if the person died without a will. In North Carolina this varies from one-half to all of the estate, depending upon whether there are any children.

Joint tenancy. A type of property ownership by two of more persons., in which if one owner dies, that owner's interest goes to the other joint owners (*not* to the deceased owner's heirs).

Legacy. Real property left to someone in a will. A person who is entitled to a legacy is called a *legatee*.

Living will. A document expressing the writer's desires regarding how medical care is to be handled in the event the writer is not able to express his or her wishes concerning the use of life-prolonging medical procedures.

Personal representative. A person appointed by the court, or in a will, to oversee distribution of the property of someone who has died. This includes both an administrator (who is appointed by the court) and an executor (who is appointed in a will).

Probate. The process of settling the estate of a deceased person through the probate court.

Residue. The property that is left over in an estate after all specific bequests and devises.

Specific bequest or devise. A gift in a will of a specific item of property, or a specific amount of money.

Tenancy by the entireties. A type of property ownership by a married couple, in which if one of the spouse's dies, his or her interest passes to the surviving spouse automatically. This is generally the same as joint tenancy, except that it is only between a husband and wife.

Tenancy in common. A type of property ownership by two or more people, in which if one owner dies, his or her interest passes to his or her heirs (not to the other joint owners).

Testate. With a will. A person who dies with a will is said to have "died testate."

Testator. (Testatrix, if female.) A person who makes a will.

There are two things in which men, in other things wise enough, do usually miscarry; in putting off the making of their wills and their repentance until it is too late.
—Tillotson

Do You Need a North Carolina Will? 2

What a Will Can Do

BENEFICIARIES

A will allows you to decide who gets your property, including land and personal items, after your death. You can give specific personal items to certain persons and decide which of your friends or relatives deserve a greater share of your estate. You may leave gifts to schools, churches, and other charities. It is, after all, your property.

PERSONAL REPRESENTATIVES

A will allows you to decide who will be the *personal representative* of your estate. A personal representative is the person that gathers your assets and distributes them to the beneficiaries. Personal representatives were formerly called *executors*. With a will you can provide that your personal representative does not have to post a surety bond with the court in order to serve and this can save your estate money. A *surety bond* is an insurance payment made by your estate to allow your personal representative to serve and do as you asked.

GUARDIAN

A will allows you to choose a guardian for your minor children. This way, you can avoid fights among relatives and make sure the best person raises your children. You may also appoint separate guardians over your children and over their money. That way, a second person can keep an eye on how the money belonging to the children is being spent.

PROTECTING HEIRS

You can set up a trust to provide that your property is not distributed immediately. Many people feel that their children would not be ready to handle large sums of money at the age of eighteen. A will can direct that the money is held until the children are twenty-one, twenty-five, or older.

MINIMIZING TAXES

If your estate is over $600,000 (this amount will increase to $1,000,000 over the next ten years) then it will be subject to federal estate taxes. If you wish to lower those taxes, for example by making gifts to charities, you can do so through a will. However, such estate planning is beyond the scope of this book and you should consult a book on estate planning or an attorney for further information.

WHAT IF YOU DO NOT HAVE A WILL?

If you do not have a will, the North Carolina Intestate Succession Act (c. 29) states that your property shall be distributed as follows:

- If you leave a spouse and two or more children or their descendants, then your spouse gets $15,000 in personal property plus one-third of the balance, and your children and grandchildren get two-thirds of the balance.

- If you leave a spouse and only one child or his or her descendants, then the spouse gets $15,000 in personal property plus one-half the balance and the child or its descendants get one-half the balance.

- If you leave children or their descendants but no spouse, then all of your property goes to your children or their descendants.

- If you leave a spouse and one or more parents but no children, then the spouse receives one-half of your real estate, $25,000 of your personal property plus one-half of the balance, and your parent or parents get one-half your real estate plus one-half of the balance of the personal property.

- If you leave a mother and/or father but no spouse or children or grandchildren, your parents receive all of your property.

- If you leave a spouse, and a brother and/or sister but no parents or children, your spouse receives all of your property.

- If you leave brothers and/or sisters but no spouse, parents, children or grandchildren, your brothers and/or sisters receive your property.

- If you leave grandparents or their descendants, but no spouse, children, grandchildren, parents. brothers or sisters, then half goes to your maternal grandparents or their descendants and half to your paternal grandparents or their descendants.

Is Your Out-of-State Will Valid in North Carolina?

A will that is valid in another state would probably be valid to pass property in North Carolina. Before such a will could be accepted by North Carolina, additional work may be required including locating the witnesses out-of-state who witnessed your signature on the will. Because of the expense and delay of having problems in finding out-of-state witnesses, it is advisable to execute a new will after moving to North Carolina.

North Carolina allows a will to be *self-proved* so that the witnesses never have to be called in to take an oath in court before the Clerk of Court to show that your will is valid with your signature. With special self-proving language in your will, the witnesses take an oath at the time of signing and never have to be seen again. This procedure is set out on the forms section and should be completed and attached to your will.

Who Can Make a North Carolina Will?

Any person who is eighteen or more years of age and of sound mind may make a will in North Carolina.

Are There Different Kinds of Wills in North Carolina?

Yes. Real estate and personal property may be passed at death to others by a witnessed will or a handwritten will. Personal property may be passed to others by an oral will. All three types of wills have special rules to make them legal and enforceable after your death.

What Is a Witnessed Will?

A *witnessed will* is a will that is hand-printed, typed, or on a form signed by the maker, and witnessed by at least two persons to legally pass your property at your death. It is referred to as an *attested will*.

What is a Handwritten or Holographic Will?

A *handwritten* or *holographic* will is a will written completely in the handwriting of the maker, signed by the maker, and found after death among valuable papers or in a safe deposit box. It does not have to be witnessed. It may, however, be witnessed and processed as a self-proving will.

What Is an Oral Will?

An *oral will* can only be made by a person in his last sickness and about to die, and who then does die. The following requirements must be met: it must be stated to be an oral will by the maker; it must be before two witnesses together at the same time with the maker; and it can only apply to personal property.

Should I Use an Oral Will?

It is not recommended that you rely on an oral will. You should plan what you want to happen to your property at a time when you are at your best, not on your deathbed.

What a Will Cannot Do

A will cannot direct that anything illegal be done and it cannot put unreasonable conditions on a gift. A provision that your daughter gets all of your property if she divorces her husband would be ignored by the court. She would get the property with no conditions attached. You can put some conditions in your will, but to be sure they are enforceable, you should consult with an attorney.

A will cannot leave money or property to an animal because animals cannot legally own property. If you wish to care for an animal after your death you should leave it in trust or to a friend whom you know will care for the animal.

Who Can Make Their Own Will?

The wills in this book will pass your property whether your estate is $1,000 or $100,000,000. However, if your estate is over $600,000 then you might be able to avoid estate taxes by using a trust or other tax-saving device. The larger your estate the more you can save on estate taxes by doing more complicated planning. If you have a large estate and are concerned about estate taxes you should consult an estate planning attorney or a book on estate planning.

Who Should Not Make Their Own Will?

Will Contest	If you expect that there may be a fight over your estate or that someone might contest your will's validity, you should consult a lawyer. If you leave less than the statutory share of your estate to your spouse or if you leave one or more of your children out of your will, it is likely that someone will contest your will.
Complicated Estates	If you are the beneficiary of a trust or have any complications in your legal relationships, you may need special provisions in your will.
Blind or Unable to Write	A person who is blind or who can sign only with an "X" should also consult a lawyer about the proper way to make and execute a will.
Estates Over $600,000	If you expect to have over $600,000 (this amount will rise to $1,000,000 over the next ten years) at the time of your death, you may want to consult with a CPA or tax attorney regarding tax consequences.
Conditions	If you wish to put some sort of conditions or restrictions on the property you leave, you should consult a lawyer. For example, if you want to leave money to your brother only if he quits smoking, or to a hospital only if they name a wing in your honor, you should consult an attorney to be sure that your conditions are valid.

What you leave at your death let it be without controversy, else the lawyer will be your heirs.
—F. Osborn

How to Make a Simple Will 3

Identifying Parties in Your Will

PEOPLE
When making your will, it is important to clearly identify the persons you name as your beneficiaries. In some families, names differ only by middle initial or by Jr., or Sr. Be sure to check everyone's name before you make your will. You can also add your relationship to the beneficiary, and their location, such as, "my cousin, John Jones of Jacksonville, North Carolina."

ORGANIZATIONS
The same applies to organizations and charities. For example, there is more than one group using the words "cancer society" or "heart association" in their names. Be sure to get the correct name of the group that you intend to leave your gift.

SPOUSE AND CHILDREN
You should mention your spouse and children in your will even if you do not leave them any property. That is to show that you are of sound mind and do know who your heirs are.

Personal Property

HANDWRITTEN LIST
Because people acquire and dispose of personal property so often, it is not advisable to list it in the will. North Carolina allows you to include

a handwritten list with your will that can divide your personal property if the list is referred to in the will. This only applies to *tangible personal property* such as watches, photos, cars, furniture, jewelry, etc. It does not include money, stocks, bonds, or real estate. By using a list you have the flexibility to make changes when you buy or sell property, such as buying a new car, necklace, or antique desk.

Real Estate

Title to land and houses in North Carolina can be passed by will, by deed, and without a will at your death. You should clearly state in your will the intended next owner of your land. Property passed from one generation to another without clear thinking ends up as *heir property* with multiple owners and no control. Eventually, this land is sold off and the costs of selling can be high.

Example
☛ When Jake died he wanted the family farm to go his children so he did not leave a will. At his death, he was survived by four children and sixteen grandchildren. Each of his children received one-fifth of the farm. Five of his grandchildren took the other one-fifth of their dead father's share giving them each a one-twenty-fifth share of the farm. Now nine people own the farm and all want something different.

Specific Bequests

Occasionally a person will want to leave a little something to a friend or charity and the rest to the family. This can be done with a *specific bequest* such as "$1,000 to my dear friend Martha Jones." Of course there could be a problem if, at the time of a person's death, there wasn't anything left after the specific bequests.

EXAMPLE ☛ At the time of making his will, Todd had $1,000,000 in assets. He felt generous so he left $50,000 to a local hospital, $50,000 to a local group that took care of homeless animals and the rest to his children. But several years later the stock market crashed and he committed suicide by jumping off a bridge. His estate at the time was worth only $110,000 so after the above specific bequests, the legal fees, and expenses of probate, there was nothing left for his five children.

Another problem with specific bequests is that some of the property may be worth considerably more or less at death than when the will was made.

EXAMPLE ☛ Joe wanted his children to equally share his estate. His will left his son his stocks (worth $500,000 at the time) and his daughter $500,000 in cash. By the time of Joe's death the stock was only worth $100,000.

He should have left "fifty percent" of his estate to each child. If giving certain things to certain people is an important part of your estate plan, you can give specific items to specific persons, but remember to make changes if your assets change.

JOINT BENEFICIARIES
Be careful about leaving one item of personal property to more than one person. For example if you leave something to your son and his wife, what would happen if they divorce. Even if you leave something to two of your own siblings, what if they can't agree about who will have possession of it? Whenever possible, leave property to one person.

TAX NOTE
Section 663 of the Internal Revenue Code excludes specific bequests of tangible personal property from the estate. If your estate is over $600,000 you may want to consult a tax advisor about taking advantage of this provision.

Remainder Clause

One of the most important clauses in a will is the *remainder clause*. This is the clause that says something like "all the rest of my property I leave to..." This clause makes sure that the will disposes of all property owned at the time of death and that nothing is forgotten.

In a simple will the best way to distribute property is to put it all in the remainder clause. In the first example in the above section, Todd's problem would have been avoided if his will had read as follows: "The rest, residue and remainder of my estate I leave, five percent to ABC Hospital, five percent to XYZ Animal Welfare League and ninety percent to be divided equally among my children..."

Alternate Beneficiaries

You should always provide for an alternate beneficiary in case the first one dies before you do and you do not have a chance to make out a new will.

Survivors or Descendants Suppose your will leaves your property to your sister and brother but your brother predeceases you. Should his share go to your sister or to your brother's children or grandchildren?

If you are giving property to two or more persons and if you want it all to go to the other if one of them dies, then you would specify "or the survivor of them."

If, on the other hand, you want the property to go to the children of the deceased person you should state in your will, "or their lineal descendants." This would include his or her children and grandchildren.

If you decide you want it to go to your brother's children and grandchildren, you must next decide if an equal share should go to each family or to each person. For example, if your brother leaves three grandchildren, one of which is an only child of his daughter and the other who are the children of his son, should all grandchildren get equal shares, or should each one take their parent's share?

FAMILY OF PERSON

When you want each family to get an equal share it is called *per stirpes*. When you want each person to get an equal share it is called *per capita*. Most of the wills in this book use per stirpes because that is the most common way property is left. If you wish to leave your property per capita then you can rewrite the will with this change.

EXAMPLE

☞ Alice leaves her property to her two daughters, Mary and Pat in equal shares, or to their lineal descendants per stirpes. Both daughters die before Alice. Mary leaves one child, Pat leaves two children. In this case Mary's child would get half of the estate and Pat's children would split the other half of the estate. If Alice had specified per capita instead of per stirpes then each child would have gotten one-third of the estate.

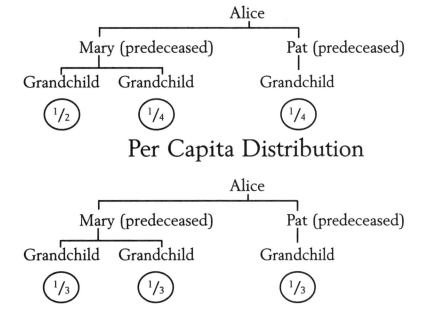

There are fourteen different will forms in this book that should cover the options most people want, but you may want to divide your property slightly differently from what is stated in these forms. If so, you can re-type the forms according to these rules, specifying whether the property should go to the survivor or the lineal descendants. If this is confusing to you, you should consider seeking the advice of an attorney.

SURVIVORSHIP

Many people put a clause in their will stating that anyone receiving property under the will must survive for thirty days (or forty-five or sixty) after the death of the person who made the will. This is so that if the two people die in the same accident there will not be two probates and the property will not go to the other party's heirs.

EXAMPLE
☛ Fred and Wilma were married and each had children by previous marriages. They didn't have survivorship clauses in their wills and they were in an airplane crash. Fred's children hired several expert witnesses and a large law firm to prove that at the time of the crash Fred lived for a few minutes longer than Wilma. That way when Wilma died first, all of her property went to Fred. When he died a few minutes later, all of Fred *and* Wilma's property went to his children, and Wilma's children got nothing.

GUARDIANS

If you have minor children you should name a guardian for them. There are two types of guardians, a guardian over the *person* and a guardian over the *property*. A guardian over the person decides where the children will live and makes the other parental decisions for them. A guardian of the property is in charge of the minor's property and inheritance. In most cases one person is appointed guardian of both the person and property. But some people prefer the children to live with one person but to have the money held by another person.

EXAMPLE   ☛ Sandra was a widow with a young daughter. She knew that if anything happened to her, her sister would be the best person to raise her daughter. But her sister was never good with money. So when Sandra made out her will she names her sister as guardian over the person of her daughter and she names her father as guardian over the estate of her daughter.

If your child's other parent is still alive and you do not want him or her to be guardian of your child, you should contact a lawyer. Naming someone other than the parent would probably not be accepted by the court if the natural parent objected.

When naming a guardian, it is always advisable to name an alternate guardian in case your first choice is unable to serve for any reason.

CHILDRENS' TRUST

When a parent dies leaving a minor child, and the child's property is held by a guardian, the guardianship ends when the child reaches the age of eighteen and all of the property is turned over to the child. Most parents do not feel their children are competent at the age of eighteen to handle large sums of money and prefer that it be held until the child is twenty-one, twenty-five, thirty, or even older.

If you wish to set up a complicated system of determining when your children should receive various amounts of your estate, or if you want the property held to a higher age than thirty-five, you should consult a lawyer to set up a trust. However, if you want a simple provision that the funds be held to a higher age than eighteen, and you have someone you trust to make decisions about paying for education or other expenses for your child or children, you can put that provision in your will as a childrens' trust.

The childrens' trust trustee can be the same person as the guardian or a different person. It is advisable to name an alternate trustee if your first choice is unable to handle it.

Personal Representative

A personal representative is the person who will be in charge of your probate. He or she will gather your assets, handle the sale of them if necessary, prepare an inventory, hire an attorney and distribute the property. This should be a person you trust, and if it is, then you can state in your will that no bond will be required to be posted by him or her. Otherwise the court will require that a surety bond be paid for by your estate to guaranty that the person is honest. You can appoint a bank to handle your estate but their fees are usually very high.

It is best to appoint a resident of your state, both because it is easier, and because a bond may be required of a non-resident even if your will waives it.

Some people like to name two persons to handle their estate to avoid jealousy, or to have them check on each other's honesty. However, this is not a good idea. It makes double work in getting the papers signed and there can be problems if they cannot agree on something.

The person handling your estate is usually entitled to some compensation. A family member will often waive the fee, but if a lot of work involved he or she may request the fee, or other family members may insist that he or she take one.

Witnesses

Witnesses should be at least eighteen-years-old and understand the seriousness of the documents you are asking them to sign. A will must be witnessed by two persons to be valid in North Carolina and all other states, except for Vermont which require three. All of the forms in this book, however, are set up for three witnesses. If you own property in Vermont, then you should use three witnesses. In North Carolina, a will that is entirely handwritten is valid if there are no witnesses, but in some states this type of will would be invalid without witnesses. If you own property or may, at the time of your death, own property in another state, use three witnesses and the notary form referred to as the *self-proving form*.

The witnesses should not be people who are beneficiaries of your will. A beneficiary will not be allowed to receive anything under the will, if they are a witness to your signature.

SELF-PROVING CLAUSE

A will only needs two witnesses to be legal, but it is highly recommended that you include a notarized *self-proving* clause to the will. This clause is usually on a separate sheet attached to your will and it is signed and notarized at the same time your will is signed and witnessed.

If a will is accompanied by a notarized self-proving clause then it may be admitted to probate without delay and without further contacting the witnesses.

Without a self-proving clause your will cannot be admitted to probate until the court determines that it is valid. This can mean the witnesses must be located and asked to sign an oath, or if the witnesses are dead someone may have to verify your handwriting.

DISINHERITING SOMEONE

Because it may result in your will being challenged in court, you should not make your own will if you intend to disinherit someone who is your natural heir. However, you may wish to leave one child less than another because you already made a gift to that child, or perhaps that child needs the money more than the other.

If you do give more to one child than to another, then you should state your reasons to show that you thought out your plan. Otherwise the one who received less might argue that you didn't realize what you were doing and were not competent to make a will.

Funeral Arrangements

There is no harm in stating your preferences in your will, but in most states directions for a funeral are not legally enforceable and many times a will is not found until after the funeral. Therefore it is better to tell your family about your wishes or to make prior arrangements yourself.

Forms

There are several different forms included in this book for easy use. You can either cut them out or photocopy them, or you can retype them on plain paper.

Cautions

Your will should have no white-outs or erasures. If for some reason it is impossible to make a will without corrections, they should be initialed by you and both witnesses. If there are two or more pages, they should be fastened together and they should state at the bottom, "Page 1 of 3," "Page 2 of 3," etc. Each page should be initialed by you and by the witnesses.

One eye-witness is worth more than ten who tell what they have heard.
—Plautus, c. 254 - 184 B.C.

How to Execute Your Will 4

The signing of a will is a serious legal event and must be done properly or the will may be declared invalid. Preferably, it should be done in a private room without distraction. All parties must watch each other sign and no one should leave the scene until all have signed.

Example
- Ebenezer was bedridden in a small room. His will was brought in to him to sign, but the witnesses could not actually see his hand signing because a dresser was in the way. His will was ignored by the court and his property went to two persons who were not in his will.

Procedure

To be sure your will is valid, you should follow these rules:

- You must state to your witnesses: *This is my will. I have read it and I understand it and this is how I want it to read. I want you people to be my witnesses.* Contrary to popular belief, you do not have to read it to the witnesses or to let them read it.

- You must date your will and sign your name at the end in ink exactly as it is printed in the will, and you should initial each page as both witnesses watch.

- You and the other witness must watch as each witness signs in ink and initials each page.

As explained in the last chapter it is important to attach a self-proving clause to your will. This means that you will need to have a notary public present to watch everyone sign. If it is impossible to have a notary present, your will will still be valid, but the probate process may be delayed.

After your witnesses have signed as attesting witnesses under your name, you and they should sign the self-proving page and the notary should notarize it. The notary should not be one of your two witnesses.

It is a good idea to make at least one copy of your will, but you should not personally sign the copies or have them notarized. The reason for this is if you cancel or destroy your will, someone may produce a copy and have it probated. Also, if you lose or destroy a copy of your will, a court may assume you intended to revoke the original.

EXAMPLE ☞ Michael typed out a copy of his will and made two photocopies. He had the original and both copies signed and notarized. He then gave the original to his sister who was to be his personal representative and kept the two copies. Upon his death the two copies were not found among his papers. Because these copies were in his possession and not found, it was assumed that he destroyed them. A court ruled that by destroying them he must have intended to revoke the original will and his property went to persons not listed in his will.

If someone made a mistake he would drawl, "Hell, that's why they make erasers."
—Clarence Darrow

AFTER YOU SIGN YOUR WILL 5

STORING YOUR WILL

Your will should be kept in a place safe from fire and easily accessible to your heirs. Your personal representative should know of its whereabouts. It can be kept in a home safe, fire box, or in a safe deposit box in a bank. Although a safe deposit box in a bank is sealed at death in North Carolina, it is easy to get a will out of a deceased person's safe deposit box.

If you are close to your children and can trust them explicitly, then you could allow one of them to keep the will in his or her safe deposit box. However, if you later decide to limit that child's share there could be a problem.

EXAMPLE ☛ Diane made out her will giving her property to her two children equally and gave it to her older child, Bill, to hold. Years later Bill moved away and her younger child, Mary took care of her by coming over every day. Diane made a new will giving most her property to Mary. Upon Diane's death Bill came to town and found the new will in Diane's house, but he destroyed it an probated the old will which gave him half the property.

Wills are not filed anywhere publicly until after a person's death. No one has to know what you have put in your will while you are alive. This allows you to change your will depending on your life changes, asset changes, and wishes. Will attorneys frequently offer to store documents at their office safe deposit box at no charge. This way he or she will likely be contacted at the time of death and will be in a good position to do the lucrative probate work.

Revoking Your Will

The usual way to revoke a will is to execute a new one that states that it revokes all previously made wills. To revoke a will without making a new one, one can tear, burn, cancel, deface, obliterate, or destroy it, as long as this is done with the intention of revoking it. If this is done accidentally, the will is not legally revoked.

Example ☛ Ralph tells his son Clyde to go to the basement safe and tear up his (Ralph's) will. If Clyde does not tear it up in Ralph's presence it is probably not effectively revoked.

What if you change your will by drafting a new one and later decide you don't like the changes and want to go back to your old will? Can you destroy the new one and revive the old one? NO! Once you execute a new will revoking an old will, you cannot revive the old one unless you execute a new document stating that you intend to revive the old will. In other words, you really should execute a new will.

Changing Your Will

You should not make any changes on your will after it has been signed. If you wish to change some provision of your will, you can do it by executing a document called a *codicil*. A person may make an unlimited number of codicils to a will, but each one must be executed with the same formality of a will and should be self-proved. Therefore, unless your will is very long, it is usually better to just prepare a new will than to prepare codicils.

To prepare a codicil, use Form 18 and then use Form 19 to make it self-proved.

Confidence in others' honesty is no light testimony of one's own integrity.
—Michel de Montaigne

How to Make a Living Will 6

A living will is not a videotape of a person making a will. It has nothing to do with the usual type of will that distributes property after death. A *living will* is a document by which a person declares that he or she does not want artificial life support systems used if he or she becomes terminally ill. In North Carolina, it is called a Declaration of a Desire for a Natural Death.

Modern science can often keep a body alive even if the brain is permanently dead, or if the person is in constant pain. In 1977, North Carolina passed a law that allowed a living will for the first time. Under this law a living will can be signed at any time. It must be signed in front of two witnesses and a notary public. Certain people cannot witness this document. These persons include relatives, doctors, and persons working for doctors. The North Carolina form lists those persons unable to be witnesses.

A living will form is included in appendix A of this book as Form 20. This is the form included in North Carolina law. A living will does not have to be on this form to be legal, but it is always better to use forms which are provided by legislature than to make up your own. A shorter version can be used as long as it expresses the intention of the person to not have artificial life prolonging procedures if he or she has a terminal condition.

Behold, I do not give lectures or a little charity, When I give I give myself.
—Walt Whitman, Leaves of Grass

How to Make Anatomical Gifts 7

Since 1969, North Carolina has allowed its residents to donate their bodies or organs for research or transplantation. Consent may be given by a relative of a deceased person, but because relatives are often in shock or too upset to make such a decision, it is better to have one's intent made clear before death. This can be done by a statement in a will or by another signed document such as the Anatomical Gift Document or a Uniform Donor Card. The gift may be of all or part of one's body and it may be made to a specific person such as a physician or an ill relative, or to a hospital. You may also designate your intention to be an Organ Donor on your North Carolina driver's license.

The document (will, anatomical gift form or card) making the donation must be signed by the donor (person making the gift) before two witnesses, who must also sign in each other's presence. If the donor cannot sign then the document may be signed for him at his direction in the presence of the witnesses.

The donor may designate in the document which doctor will carry out the procedure at death. The donor can specify the donee (person receiving the gift) and what body parts may be used, such as eyes and kidneys, or may specify that all body parts may be used. This directive can also state that your body can be used by a hospital, doctor, dentist, medical school, dental school, or other university for education or research.

If the anatomical gift document or will has been delivered to a specific donee it may be amended or revoked by the donor in the following ways:

1. By executing and delivering a signed statement to the donee.

2. By an oral statement to two witnesses communicated to the donee.

3. By an oral statement during a terminal illness made to an attending physician and communicated to the donee.

4. By a signed document found on the person of the donor or in his or her effects.

If an anatomical gift document has not been delivered to a donee it may be revoked by any of the above methods or by destruction, cancellation, or mutilation of the document. It may also be revoked in the same method a will is revoked as described on page 38.

It is helpful to inform your close relatives of your wish to make an anatomical gift. Finding this out at your death may be difficult for some family members.

An Anatomical Gift form and Uniform Donor Cards are included in appendix A as Forms 21 and 22. They must be signed in the presence of two witnesses, who must also sign.

Appendix A
Sample Filled-in Forms

The following pages contain some of the forms from appendix B, that have been filled-in for fictional people. These sample forms should give you an idea of how your forms should look once you have completed them. Please note that to save space we have only included one sample of the self-proving affidavit although it should be used with all wills. The forms included in this appendix are:

9. **Simple Will**—Spouse and Adult Children. John Smith is giving all of his property to his wife, Barbara; but if she dies first, then all of his property goes to his three adult children, Amy, Beamy, and Seamy. (Page 47.)

11. **Simple Will**—No spouse, property to minor children with two guardians. (Page 49.)

15. **Simple Will**—No spouse, no children. (Page 51.)

17. **Self-Proved Will Affidavit**—This page would be attached to Woodrow Allen's will, and would be witnessed and notarized. (Page 53.)

18. **Codicil to Will**—Larry Lowe is changing his will to reduce the amount of the specific bequest to his daughter, Mildred, form $5,000 to $1,000. (Page 54.)

20. **Living Will**—This is a Declaration of a Desire for Natural Death (also known as a living will) executed by John Smith. (Page 55.)

21. **Anatomical Gift**—This form can be used to provide for your wishes about leaving any or all of your body parts for organ donation, education or medical research. (Page 56.)

Form 9. Simple Will—Spouse and Adult children (to spouse and children)

Last Will and Testament

I, __John Smith__ a resident of __Dare__ County, North Carolina do hereby make, publish, and declare this to be my Last Will and Testament, hereby revoking any and all Wills and Codicils heretofore made by me.

FIRST: I direct that all my just debts and funeral expenses be paid out of my estate as soon after my death as is practicable.

SECOND: I may leave a statement or list giving certain items of my personal property to specific people. Any such statement or list in existence at my death shall be final.

THIRD: I give, devise, and bequeath all my estate, real, personal, and mixed, of whatever kind and wherever situated, of which I may die seized or possessed, or in which I may have any interest or over which I may have any power of appointment or testamentary disposition, as follows:
__50__ % to my spouse, __Barbara Smith__ and
__50__ % to my children, __Amy Smith, Beamy Smith and Seamy Smith------__
in equal shares or to their lineal descendants per stirpes.

FOURTH: In the event that any beneficiary fails to survive me by thirty days, then this will shall take effect as if that person had predeceased me.

FIFTH: I hereby nominate, constitute, and appoint __Barbara Smith__ as Personal Representative of this, my Last Will and Testament. In the event that such named person is unable or unwilling to serve at any time or for any reason then I nominate, constitute, and appoint __Reginald Smith__ as Personal Representative in the place and stead of the person first named herein. It is my will and I direct that my Personal Representative shall not be required to furnish a bond for the faithful performance of his or her duties in any jurisdiction, any provision of law to the contrary notwithstanding and I give my Personal Representative full power to administer my estate, including the power to settle claims, pay debts, and sell, lease or exchange real and personal property without court order.

IN WITNESS WHEREOF I declare this to be my Last Will and Testament and execute it willingly as my free and voluntary act for the purposes expressed herein and I am of legal age and sound mind and make this under no constraint or undue influence, this __24__ day of __December__, __2002__.

John Smith L.S.

The foregoing instrument was on said date subscribed at the end thereof by __John Smith__, the above named Testator who signed, published, and declared this instrument to be his/her Last Will and Testament in the presence of us and each of us, who thereupon at his/her request, in his/her presence, and in the presence of each other, have

Initials: __J.S.__ (Testator) __W.W.__ (Witness) __B.B.__ (Witness) __R.R.__ (Witness) Page __1__ of __2__

hereunto subscribed our names as witnesses thereto. We understand this to be his/her will and to the best of our knowledge testator is of legal age, of sound mind, and under no constraint or undue influence.

William W. Wilson residing at *123 Main St. Greenville, NC 27858*

Barbara Brown residing at *61 State St., Greenville, NC 27858*

Robert R. Robertson residing at *8917 Green St., Greenville, NC 27858*

Form 11. Simple Will—No Spouse—Minor Children—Two Guardians

Last Will and Testament

I, __John Doe__ a resident of __Windsor__ County, North Carolina do hereby make, publish, and declare this to be my Last Will and Testament, hereby revoking any and all Wills and Codicils heretofore made by me.

FIRST: I direct that all my just debts and funeral expenses be paid out of my estate as soon after my death as is practicable.

SECOND: I may leave a statement or list giving certain items of my personal property to specific people. Any such statement or list in existence at my death shall be final.

THIRD: I give, devise, and bequeath all my estate, real, personal, and mixed, of whatever kind and wherever situated, of which I may die seized or possessed, or in which I may have any interest or over which I may have any power of appointment or testamentary disposition, to my children __James Doe, Mary Doe, Larry Doe, Barry Doe, Carrie Doe, and Moe Doe_____,
plus any afterborn or adopted children in equal shares or to their lineal descendants per stirpes.

FOURTH: In the event that any beneficiary fails to survive me by thirty days, then this will shall take effect as if that person had predeceased me.

FIFTH: In the event any of my children have not attained the age of 18 years at the time of my death, I hereby nominate, constitute, and appoint __Herbert Doe__ as guardian over the person of any of my children who have not reached the age of majority at the time of my death. In the event that said guardian is unable or unwilling to serve then I nominate, constitute, and appoint __Tom Doe__ as guardian. Said guardian to serve without bond or surety.

SIXTH: In the event any of my children have not attained the age of 18 years at the time of my death, I hereby nominate, constitute, and appoint __Clarence Doe__ as guardian over the property of any of my children who have not reached the age of majority at the time of my death. In the event that said guardian is unable or unwilling to serve then I nominate, constitute, and appoint __Englebert Doe__ as guardian. Said guardian to serve without bond or surety.

SEVENTH: I hereby nominate, constitute, and appoint __Clarence Doe__ as Personal Representative of this, my Last Will and Testament. In the event that such named person is unable or unwilling to serve at any time or for any reason then I nominate, constitute, and appoint __Englebert Doe__ as Personal Representative in the place and stead of the person first named herein. It is my will and I direct that my Personal Representative shall not be required to furnish a bond for the faithful performance of his or her duties in any jurisdiction, any provision of law to the contrary notwithstanding and I give my Personal Representative full power to administer my estate, including the power to settle claims, pay debts, and sell, lease or exchange real and personal property without court order.

IN WITNESS WHEREOF I declare this to be my Last Will and Testament and execute it willingly as my free and voluntary act for the purposes expressed herein and I am of legal age and sound mind and make this under no constraint or undue influence, this <u>26th</u> day of <u>January</u>, <u>2001</u>.

<u>   *John Doe*   </u>L.S.

The foregoing instrument was on said date subscribed at the end thereof by <u> John Doe </u>, the above named Testator who signed, published, and declared this instrument to be his/her Last Will and Testament in the presence of us and each of us, who thereupon at his/her request, in his/her presence, and in the presence of each other, have hereunto subscribed our names as witnesses thereto. We understand this to be his/her will and to the best of our knowledge testator is of legal age, of sound mind, and under no constraint or undue influence.

<u>*Patricia P. Patterson*   </u> residing at <u>*123 Oak St. Winston Salem, NC 27812*</u>

<u>*Thomas T. Thompson*   </u> residing at <u>*234 Elm St., Winston Salem, NC 27812*</u>

<u>*Joseph J. Josephston*   </u> residing at <u>*456 Cherry St., Winston Salem, NC 27812*</u>

Form 15. Simple Will—No spouse and no children (to survivor)

Last Will and Testament

I, __Woodrow Allen__ a resident of __Oxford__ County, North Carolina do hereby make, publish, and declare this to be my Last Will and Testament, hereby revoking any and all Wills and Codicils heretofore made by me.

FIRST: I direct that all my just debts and funeral expenses be paid out of my estate as soon after my death as is practicable.

SECOND: I may leave a statement or list giving certain items of my personal property to specific people. Any such statement or list in existence at my death shall be final.

THIRD: I give, devise, and bequeath all my estate, real, personal, and mixed, of whatever kind and wherever situated, of which I may die seized or possessed, or in which I may have any interest or over which I may have any power of appointment or testamentary disposition, to the following: __100 per cent to Susie Allen or her lineal descendants, per stirpes.__

~~or to the survivor of them~~.

FOURTH: In the event that any beneficiary fails to survive me by thirty days, then this will shall take effect as if that person had predeceased me.

FIFTH: I hereby nominate, constitute, and appoint __Susie Allen__ as Personal Representative of this, my Last Will and Testament. In the event that such named person is unable or unwilling to serve at any time or for any reason then I nominate, constitute, and appoint __Louie Lassiter__ as Personal Representative in the place and stead of the person first named herein. It is my will and I direct that my Personal Representative shall not be required to furnish a bond for the faithful performance of his or her duties in any jurisdiction, any provision of law to the contrary notwithstanding and I give my Personal Representative full power to administer my estate, including the power to settle claims, pay debts, and sell, lease or exchange real and personal property without court order.

IN WITNESS WHEREOF I declare this to be my Last Will and Testament and execute it willingly as my free and voluntary act for the purposes expressed herein and I am of legal age and sound mind and make this under no constraint or undue influence, this __29__ day of __January__, __1999__.

Woodrow Allen L.S.

The foregoing instrument was on said date subscribed at the end thereof by __Woodrow Allen__, the above named Testator who signed, published, and declared this instrument to be his/her Last Will and Testament in the presence of us and each of us, who thereupon at his/her request, in his/her presence, and in the presence of each other, have hereunto subscribed our names as witnesses thereto. We understand this to be his/her will and to the

Initials: __W.A.__ Testator __J.J.__ Witness __P.P.__ Witness __M.M.__ Witness Page __1__ of __3__

best of our knowledge testator is of legal age, of sound mind, and under no constraint or undue influence.

James A. Jameson _____ residing at _____ 111 Jerry St. Raleigh, NC 27800

Peter B. Peterson _____ residing at _____ 2222 Shake St., Raleigh, NC 27800

Michael C. Michaelson _____ residing at _____ 555 Down St., Raleigh, NC 27800

Self-Proved Will Affidavit
(attach to Will)

STATE OF NORTH CAROLINA

COUNTY OF __Oxford__

    I, the undersigned, an officer authorized to administer oaths, certify that _____Woodrow Allen_____, the testator and _____James A. Jameson_____, _____Peter B. Peterson_____, and _____Michael C. Michaelson_____, the witnesses, whose names are signed to the attached or foregoing instrument and whose signatures appear below, having appeared before me and having been first been duly sworn, each then declared to me that: 1) the attached or foregoing instrument is the last will of the testator; 2) the testator willingly and voluntarily declared, signed and executed the will in the presence of the witnesses; 3) the witnesses signed the will upon the request of the testator, in the presence and hearing of the testator and in the presence of each other; 4) to the best knowledge of each witness, the testator was, at the time of signing, of the age of majority (or otherwise legally competent to make a will), of sound mind and memory and under no constraint or undue influence; and 5) each witness was and is competent and of proper age to witness a will.

                                        _Woodrow Allen_____ (Testator)

                                        _James A. Jameson_____ (Witness)

                                        _Peter B. Peterson_____ (Witness)

                                        _Michael C. Michaelson_____ (Witness)

Subscribed, sworn and acknowledged before me by _____Woodrow Allen_____, the testator, and by _____James A. Jameson_____, _____Peter B. Peterson_____, _____Michael C. Michaelson_____, witnesses, this __29th__ day of __January__, __1999__.

_C.U. Sine_____
Notary or other officer

Initials: __L.L.__ __J.D.__ __R.L.__ __G.W.__   Page __3__ of __3__
       Testator Witness Witness Witness

Form 18. Codicil to Will

First Codicil to the Will of

Larry Lowe

I, __Larry Lowe__, a resident of __Onslow__ County, North Carolina declare this to be the first codicil to my Last Will and Testament dated __September, 15__, __2000__.

FIRST: I hereby revoke the clause of my Will which reads as follows: __FOURTH: I hereby leave $5000.00 to my daughter Mildred.__

SECOND: I hereby add following clause to my Will: __FOURTH: I hereby leave $1000.00 to my daughter Mildred.__

THIRD: In all other respects I hereby confirm and republish my Last Will and Testament dated __December, 3__, __1998__.

IN WITNESS WHEREOF, I have signed, published and declared the foregoing instrument as and for a codicil to my Last Will and Testament, this __15th__ day of __September__, __2000__.

Larry Lowe

The foregoing instrument was on the __15th__ day of __September__, __2000__, signed at the end thereof, and at the same time published and declared by __Larry Lowe__, as and for a codicil to his/her Last Will and Testament, dated __September 15,__ __2000__, in the presence of each of us, who, this attestation clause having been read to us, did at the request of the said testator/testatrix, in his/her presence and in the presence of each other signed our names as witnesses thereto.

Roberta Lee residing at *123 Gum Branch Rd. Jacksonville, NC 27845*

Jeffersina Davis residing at *456 Sherry Ct., Jacksonville, NC 27845*

Georgina Washington residing at *888 Daniel Pl., Jacksonville, NC 27845*

Initials: __L.L.__ (Testator) __R.L.__ (Witness) __J.D.__ (Witness) __G.W.__ (Witness)

Form 20. Living Will

DECLARATION OF A DESIRE FOR NATURAL DEATH

I, John Smith, being of sound mind, desire that, as specified below, my life not be prolonged by extraordinary means or by artificial nutrition or hydration if my condition is determined to be terminal and incurable or if I am diagnosed as being in a persistent vegetative state. I am aware and understand that this writing authorizes a physician to withhold or discontinue extraordinary means or artificial nutrition or hydration, in accordance with my specifications set forth below:

(Initial any of the following, as desired:)

J.S. If my condition is determined to be terminal and incurable, I authorize the following:

_____ My physician may withhold or discontinue extraordinary means only.

J.S. In addition to withholding or discontinuing extraordinary means if such are necessary, my physician may withhold or discontinue either artificial nutrition or hydration, or both.

J.S. If my physician determines that I am in a persistent vegetative state, I authorize the following:

J.S. My physician may withhold or discontinue extraordinary means only.

J.S. In addition to withholding or discontinuing extraordinary means if such are necessary, my physician may withhold or discontinue either artificial nutrition or hydration, or both.

This the 7 day of May, 2000.

John Smith
Declarant

I hereby state that the Declarant, John Smith, being of sound mind signed the above declaration in my presence and that I am not related to the Declarant by blood or marriage and that I do not now or have a reasonable expectation that I would be entitled to any portion of the estate of the Declarant under any existing Will or Codicil of the Declarant, or as an heir under the Intestate Succession Act if the Declarant died on this date without a will. I also state that I am not the Declarant's attending physician, or an employee of the Declarant's attending physician, or an employee of a health facility in which the Declarant is a patient, or an employee of a Nursing Home or any group care home, where the Declarant resides. I further state that I do not now have any claim against the Declarant.

Frederick Farkle
Witness
Francis Farkle
Witness

NORTH CAROLINA
COUNTY OF Asheville

CERTIFICATE

I, a Notary Public in and for the State of North Carolina, hereby certify that John Smith, the Declarant, appeared before me and swore to me and to the witnesses in my presence that this instrument is his/her Declaration of a Desire For a Natural Death, and that he/she had willingly and voluntarily made and executed it as his/her free act and deed for the purposes expressed in it.

I further certify that Frederick Farkle and Francis Farkle, witnesses, appeared before me and swore that they witnessed John Smith, the declarant, sign the attached declaration, believing him/her to be of sound mind; and also swore that at the time they witnessed the declaration (i) they were not related within the third degree to the Declarant or to any Declarant's spouse, and (ii) that they did not now or have a reasonable expectation that they would be entitled to any portion of the Estate of the Declarant upon the Declarant's death under any Will of the Declarant, or Codicil thereto, then existing or under the Intestate Succession Act as it provides at that time, (iii) they were not a physician attending the Declarant, or any employee of an attending physician, or an employee of a health facility in which the Declarant was a patient, or of a nursing home or of any group care home, in which the Declarant resided, and (iv) they did not have a claim against the Declarant. I further certify that I am satisfied as to the genuineness and due execution of the Declaration.

This the 7 day of May, 2000.

C. U. Sine
Notary Public

(NOTARY SEAL)

Instrument of Anatomical Gift

I, __John Doe__, of __Wilmington__, North Carolina, make this anatomical gift to take effect upon my death and prior to embalmment of my body, revoking all prior anatomical gift instruments made by me.

FIRST: I give the North Carolina EYE BANK of Raleigh, North Carolina, or to any eye bank serving the area in which my death occurs, both or either of my eyes for such use as the Donee may see fit with regard to all or any part of said eyes.

SECOND: I give any organ of my body (other than my eyes) to be used for any appropriate purpose and authorize any portion of my body to be transplanted to the body of any other person.

THIRD: I give my entire body to __Duke University__ Medical School, for the promotion of anatomical study and teaching or any medical school in the area in which my death occurs. I direct that after these purposes have been accomplished, (my remains OR the remainder of my body be cremated and remains) be buried in __Cedar Oaks__ Cemetery with the services of the (Priest) ~~(Minister) (Rabbi)~~ of the __Catholic__ faith.

WITNESS, I the Donor, have signed this __20th__ day of __July__, __2001__.

_____John Doe_____
(DONOR)

This instrument was signed by __John Doe__, in our presence, and in the presence of each other as witnesses, this __20th__ day of __July__, __2001__.

Jonathan O. Jones residing at _222 Surf City Rd., Wilmington, NC 27800_
Witness

Doris H. Dory residing at _333 Pebble Beach Rd., Wilmington, NC 27800_
Witness

Oliver T. Oliveston residing at _444 University Blvd., Wilmington, NC 27800_
Witness

Appendix B
Forms

The following pages contain forms that can be used to prepare a will, codicil, living will, and Uniform Donor Card. They should only be used by persons who have read this book, who do not have any complications in their legal affairs, and who understand the forms they are using. The forms may be used right out of the book, or they may be photocopied, or retyped. Two copies are included of each form.

Form 1. Asset and Beneficiary List—*Use this form to keep an accurate record of your estate as well as your beneficiaries' names and addresses.*

Form 2. Preferences List—*Use this form to let your family know of your wishes on matters not usually included in a will.*

Form 3. Simple Will—Spouse and Minor Children—One Guardian. *Use this will if you have minor children and want all your property to go to your spouse, but if your spouse dies previously, then to your minor children. It provides for one person to be guardian over your children and their estates.*

Form 4. Simple Will—Spouse and Minor Children—Two Guardians. *Use this will if you have minor children and want all your property to go to your spouse, but if your spouse dies previously, then to your minor children. It provides for two guardians, one over your children and one over their estates.*

Form 5. Simple Will—Spouse and Minor Children—Guardian and Trust. *This will should be used if you have minor children and want all your property to go to your spouse, but if your spouse dies previously, then to your minor children. It provides for one person to be guardian over your children and for either the same person or another to be trustee over their property. This will allows* your children's property to be held until they are older than eighteen rather than distributing it all to them at age eighteen.

Form 6. Simple Will—Spouse and no children. *Use this will if you want your property to go to your spouse but if your spouse predeceases you, to others or the **survivor** of the others.*

Form 7. Simple Will—Spouse and no children. *Use this will if you want your property to go to your spouse but if your spouse predeceases you, to others or the **children and grandchildren** of the others.*

Form 8. Simple Will—Spouse and Adult Children. *Use this will if you want all of your property to go to your spouse, but if your spouse dies previously, then to your children, all of whom are adults.*

Form 9. Simple Will—Spouse and Adult Children. *Use this will if you want some of your property to go to your spouse, and some of your property to your children, all of whom are adults.*

Form 10. Simple Will—No Spouse—Minor Children—One Guardian. *Use this will if you do not have a spouse and want all your property to go to your children, at least one of whom is a minor. It provides for one person to be guardian over your children and their estates.*

Form 11. Simple Will—No Spouse—Minor Children—Two Guardians. *Use this will if you do not have a spouse and want all your property to go to your children, at least one of whom is a minor. It provides for two guardians, one over your children and one over their estates.*

Form 12. Simple Will—No Spouse—Minor Children—Guardian and Trust. *Use this will if you do not have a spouse and want all your property to go to your children, at least one of whom is a minor. It provides for one person to be guardian over your children and for either that person or another to be trustee over their property. This will allows your children's property to be held until they are older than eighteen rather than distributing it all to them at age eighteen.*

Form 13. Simple Will—No Spouse—Adult Children. *This will should be used if you wish to leave your property to your adult children, or equally to each **family** if they predecease you.*

Form 14. Simple Will—No Spouse—Adult Children. *This will should be used if you wish to leave your property to your adult children, or equally to each **person** if they predecease you.*

Form 15. Simple Will—No spouse and no children. *Use this will if you have no spouse or children and want your property to go to the **survivor** of the people you name.*

Form 16. Simple Will—No spouse and no children. *Use this will if you have no spouse or children and want your property to go to the **children and grandchildren** of the people you name.*

Form 17. Self-Proved Will Page. *This affidavit should be executed by you and the witnesses to your will at the time of executing your will.*

Form 18. Codicil to Will. *This form can be used to change one section of your will. Usually it is just as easy to execute a new will, since all of the same formalities are required.*

Form 19. Self-Proved Codicil Page. *This affidavit should be executed by you and the witnesses to your will at the time of executing your codicil.*

Form 20. Living Will. *This is a document which expresses your desire to withhold certain extraordinary medical treatment should you have a terminal illness and you reach such a state that your wishes to withhold such treatment cannot be determined.*

Form 21. Instrument of Anatomical Gift. *This form is used to spell out your wishes for donation of your body or any organs.*

Form 22. Organ Donor Card. *This form is used to spell out your wishes for donation of your body or any organs and can be carried in your wallet or purse.*

How to Pick the Right Will

Follow the chart and use the form number in the black circle, then use the affidavit in the black box.

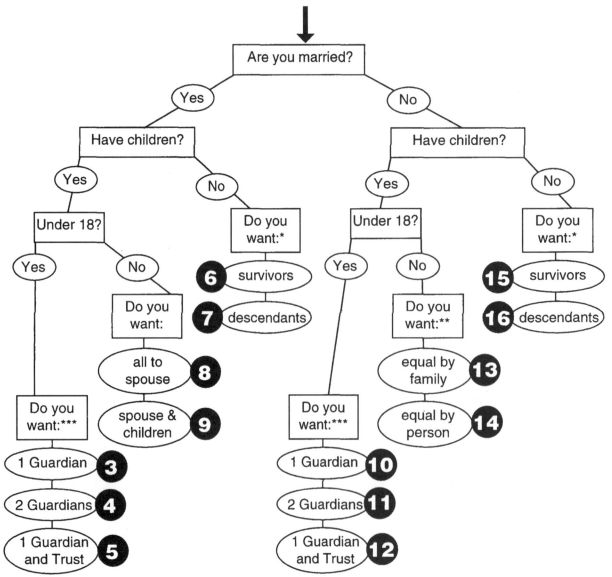

 Be sure to use Form 17, the self-proving affidavit with your will, no matter which form you use.

*For an explanation of survivors/descendants, see page 28.

**For an explanation of families/persons see page 29.

***For an explanation of childrens' guardians and trust, see page 31.

Asset and Beneficiary List

Property Inventory

Assets

Bank Accounts (checking, savings, certificates of deposit)

_____
_____
_____
_____
_____
_____
_____
_____

Real Estate

_____
_____
_____
_____
_____
_____
_____
_____

Vehicles (cars, trucks, boats, planes, RVs, etc.)

_____
_____
_____
_____
_____
_____
_____
_____

Personal Property (collections, jewelry, tools, artwork, household items, etc.)

_____
_____
_____
_____
_____
_____
_____
_____

Stocks/Bonds/Mutual Funds

Retirement Accounts (IRAs, 401(k)s, pension plans, etc.)

Receivables (mortgages held, notes, accounts receivable, personal loans)

Life Insurance

_____
_____
_____
_____
_____
_____

Other Property (trusts, partnerships, businesses, profit sharing, copyrights, etc.)

_____
_____
_____
_____
_____
_____

Liabilities

Real Estate Loans

_____
_____
_____
_____
_____
_____

Vehicle Loans

_____
_____
_____
_____
_____
_____

Other Secured Loans

_____
_____
_____
_____
_____
_____
_____
_____
_____

Unsecured Loans and Debts (taxes, child support, judgments, etc.)

_____
_____
_____
_____
_____
_____
_____
_____

Beneficiary List

_____
_____
_____
_____
_____
_____
_____
_____

Preferences List

STATEMENT OF DESIRES AND LOCATION OF PROPERTY & DOCUMENTS

I, _____, am signing this document as the expression of my desires as to the matters stated below, and to inform my family members or other significant persons of the location of certain property and documents in the event of any emergency or of my death.

1. **Funeral Desires.** It is my desire that the following arrangements be made for my funeral and disposition of remains in the event of my death (state if you have made any arrangements, such as pre-paid burial plans, cemetery plots owned, etc.):

   ❏ Burial at _____
   _____.

   ❏ Cremation at _____
   _____.

   ❏ Other specific desires: _____
   _____
   _____.

2. **Pets.** I have the following pet(s): _____
_____. The following are my desires concerning the care of said pet(s): _____
_____
_____.

4. **Notification.** I would like the following person(s) notified in the event of emergency or death (give name, address and phone number):

   _____
   _____
   _____
   _____.

5. **Location of Documents.** The following is a list of important documents, and their location:

   ❏ Last Will and Testament, dated _____. Location: _____
   _____.

   ❏ Codicil to Last Will and Testament, dated _____. Location: _____
   _____.

   ❏ Durable Power of Attorney, dated _____. Location: _____
   _____.

   ❏ Living Will, dated _____. Location: _____
   _____.

   ❏ Deed(s) to real estate (describe property location and location of deed):
   _____
   _____
   _____

- ❏ Title(s) to vehicles (cars, boats, etc.) (Describe vehicle, its location, and location of title, registration, or other documents):

  _____
  _____
  _____

- ❏ Life insurance policies (list name address & phone number of insurance company and insurance agent, policy number, and location of policy):

  _____
  _____
  _____

- ❏ Other insurance policies (list type, company & agent, policy number, and location of policy):

  _____
  _____
  _____

- ❏ Other: (list other documents such as stock certificates, bonds, certificates of deposit, etc., and their location):

  _____
  _____
  _____

6. **Location of Assets.** In addition to items readily visible in my home or listed above, I have the following assets:

   - ❏ Safe deposit box located at _____, box number _____. Key located at: _____.
   - ❏ Bank accounts (list name & address of bank, type of account, and account number):

     _____

   - ❏ Other (describe the item and give its location):

     _____
     _____
     _____
     _____
     _____

7. Other desires or information (state any desires or provide any information not given above; use additional sheets of paper if necessary):

   _____
   _____
   _____
   _____
   _____

Dated: _____

_____
Signature

Last Will and Testament

I, _____ a resident of _____ County, North Carolina do hereby make, publish, and declare this to be my Last Will and Testament, hereby revoking any and all Wills and Codicils heretofore made by me.

    FIRST: I direct that all my just debts and funeral expenses be paid out of my estate as soon after my death as is practicable.

    SECOND: I may leave a statement or list giving certain items of my personal property to specific people. Any such statement or list in existence at my death shall be final.

    THIRD: I give, devise, and bequeath all my estate, real, personal, and mixed, of whatever kind and wherever situated, of which I may die seized or possessed, or in which I may have any interest or over which I may have any power of appointment or testamentary disposition, to my spouse, _____. If my said spouse does not survive me, I give, and bequeath the said property to my children _____ _____ _____ , plus any afterborn or adopted children in equal shares.

    FOURTH: In the event that any beneficiary fails to survive me by thirty days, then this will shall take effect as if that person had predeceased me.

    FIFTH: Should my spouse not survive me, I hereby nominate, constitute, and appoint _____ as guardian over the person and estate of any of my children who have not reached the age of majority at the time of my death. In the event that said guardian is unable or unwilling to serve then I nominate, constitute, and appoint _____ as guardian. Said guardian to serve without bond or surety.

    SIXTH: I hereby nominate, constitute, and appoint _____ as Personal Representative of this, my Last Will and Testament. In the event that such named person is unable or unwilling to serve at any time or for any reason then I nominate, constitute, and appoint _____ as Personal Representative in the place and stead of the person first named herein. It is my will and I direct that my Personal Representative shall not be required to furnish a bond for the faithful performance of his or her duties in any jurisdiction, any provision of law to the contrary notwithstanding and I give my Personal Representative full power to administer my estate, including the power to settle claims, pay debts, and sell, lease or exchange real and personal property without court order.

    IN WITNESS WHEREOF I declare this to be my Last Will and Testament and execute it willingly as my free and voluntary act for the purposes expressed herein and I am of legal age and sound mind and make this under no constraint or undue influence, this _____ day of _____, _____.

Initials: _____ _____ _____ _____   Page ___ of ___
          Testator   Witness   Witness   Witness

_____L.S.

The foregoing instrument was on said date subscribed at the end thereof by _____, the above named Testator who signed, published, and declared this instrument to be his/her Last Will and Testament in the presence of us and each of us, who thereupon at his/her request, in his/her presence, and in the presence of each other, have hereunto subscribed our names as witnesses thereto. We understand this to be his/her will and to the best of our knowledge testator is of legal age, of sound mind, and under no constraint or undue influence.

_____residing at_____

_____residing at_____

_____residing at_____

Form 4. Simple Will—Spouse and Minor Children—Two Guardians

Last Will and Testament

I, _____ a resident of _____ County, North Carolina do hereby make, publish, and declare this to be my Last Will and Testament, hereby revoking any and all Wills and Codicils heretofore made by me.

FIRST: I direct that all my just debts and funeral expenses be paid out of my estate as soon after my death as is practicable.

SECOND: I may leave a statement or list giving certain items of my personal property to specific people. Any such statement or list in existence at my death shall be final.

THIRD: I give, devise, and bequeath all my estate, real, personal, and mixed, of whatever kind and wherever situated, of which I may die seized or possessed, or in which I may have any interest or over which I may have any power of appointment or testamentary disposition, to my spouse, _____. If my said spouse does not survive me, I give, and bequeath the said property to my children _____
_____
_____ ,
plus any afterborn or adopted children in equal shares.

FOURTH: In the event that any beneficiary fails to survive me by thirty days, then this will shall take effect as if that person had predeceased me.

FIFTH: Should my spouse not survive me, I hereby nominate, constitute, and appoint _____, as guardian over the person of any of my children who have not reached the age of majority at the time of my death. In the event that said guardian is unable or unwilling to serve then I nominate, constitute, and appoint _____ as guardian. Said guardian to serve without bond or surety.

SIXTH: Should my spouse not survive me, I hereby nominate, constitute, and appoint _____ as guardian over the estate of any of my children who have not reached the age of majority at the time of my death. In the event that said guardian is unable or unwilling to serve then I nominate, constitute, and appoint _____ as guardian. Said guardian to serve without bond or surety.

SEVENTH: I hereby nominate, constitute, and appoint _____ as Personal Representative of this, my Last Will and Testament. In the event that such named person is unable or unwilling to serve at any time or for any reason then I nominate, constitute, and appoint _____ as Personal Representative in the place and stead of the person first named herein. It is my will and I direct that my Personal Representative shall not be required to furnish a bond for the faithful performance of his or her duties in any jurisdiction, any provision of law to the contrary notwithstanding and I give my Personal Representative full power to administer my estate, including the power to settle claims, pay debts, and sell, lease or exchange real and personal property without court order.

Initials: _____ _____ _____ _____   Page ____ of ____
         Testator   Witness   Witness   Witness

IN WITNESS WHEREOF I declare this to be my Last Will and Testament and execute it willingly as my free and voluntary act for the purposes expressed herein and I am of legal age and sound mind and make this under no constraint or undue influence, this _____ day of _____, _____.

_____L.S.

The foregoing instrument was on said date subscribed at the end thereof by _____, the above named Testator who signed, published, and declared this instrument to be his/her Last Will and Testament in the presence of us and each of us, who thereupon at his/her request, in his/her presence, and in the presence of each other, have hereunto subscribed our names as witnesses thereto. We understand this to be his/her will and to the best of our knowledge testator is of legal age, of sound mind, and under no constraint or undue influence.

_____residing at_____

_____residing at_____

_____residing at_____

Last Will and Testament

I, _____ a resident of _____ County, North Carolina do hereby make, publish, and declare this to be my Last Will and Testament, hereby revoking any and all Wills and Codicils heretofore made by me.

FIRST: I direct that all my just debts and funeral expenses be paid out of my estate as soon after my death as is practicable.

SECOND: I may leave a statement or list giving certain items of my personal property to specific people. Any such statement or list in existence at my death shall be final.

THIRD: I give, devise, and bequeath all my estate, real, personal, and mixed, of whatever kind and wherever situated, of which I may die seized or possessed, or in which I may have any interest or over which I may have any power of appointment or testamentary disposition, to my spouse, _____. If my said spouse does not survive me, I give, and bequeath the said property to my children _____
_____
_____,
plus any afterborn or adopted children in equal shares.

FOURTH: In the event that any beneficiary fails to survive me by thirty days, then this will shall take effect as if that person had predeceased me.

FIFTH: In the event that any of my children have not reached the age of _____ years at the time of my death, then the share of any such child shall be held in a separate trust by _____ for such child.

The trustee shall use the income and that part of the principal of the trust as is, in the trustee's sole discretion, necessary or desirable to provide proper housing, medical care, food, clothing, entertainment and education for the trust beneficiary, considering the beneficiary's other resources. Any income that is not distributed shall be added to the principal. Additionally, the trustee shall have all powers conferred by the law of the state having jurisdiction over this trust, as well as the power to pay from the assets of the trust reasonable fees necessary to administer the trust.

The trust shall terminate when the child reaches the age specified above and the remaining assets distributed to the child, unless they have been exhausted sooner. In the event the child dies prior to the termination of the trust, then the assets shall pass to the estate of the child. The interests of the beneficiary under this trust shall not be assignable and shall be free from the claims of creditors to the full extent allowed by law.

In the event the said trustee is unable or unwilling to serve for any reason, then I nominate, constitute, and appoint _____ as alternate trustee. No bond shall be required of either trustee in any jurisdiction and this trust shall be administered without court supervision as allowed by law.

SIXTH: Should my spouse not survive me, I hereby nominate, constitute, and appoint_____as guardian over the person and estate of any of my children who have not reached the age of majority at the time of my death. In the event that said guardian is unable or unwilling to serve then I nominate, constitute, and appoint_____ as guardian.

SEVENTH: I hereby nominate, constitute, and appoint _____ as Personal Representative of this, my Last Will and Testament. In the event that such named person is unable or unwilling to serve at any time or for any reason then I nominate, constitute, and appoint _____ as Personal Representative in the place and stead of the person first named herein. It is my will and I direct that my Personal Representative shall not be required to furnish a bond for the faithful performance of his or her duties in any jurisdiction, any provision of law to the contrary notwithstanding and I give my Personal Representative full power to administer my estate, including the power to settle claims, pay debts, and sell, lease or exchange real and personal property without court order.

IN WITNESS WHEREOF I declare this to be my Last Will and Testament and execute it willingly as my free and voluntary act for the purposes expressed herein and I am of legal age and sound mind and make this under no constraint or undue influence, this _____ day of _____, _____.

_____L.S.

The foregoing instrument was on said date subscribed at the end thereof by _____, the above named Testator who signed, published, and declared this instrument to be his/her Last Will and Testament in the presence of us and each of us, who thereupon at his/her request, in his/her presence, and in the presence of each other, have hereunto subscribed our names as witnesses thereto. We understand this to be his/her will and to the best of our knowledge testator is of legal age, of sound mind, and under no constraint or undue influence.

_____residing at_____

_____residing at_____

_____residing at_____

Form 6. Simple Will—Spouse and no children (survivor)

Last Will and Testament

I, _____ a resident of _____ County, North Carolina do hereby make, publish, and declare this to be my Last Will and Testament, hereby revoking any and all Wills and Codicils heretofore made by me.

FIRST: I direct that all my just debts and funeral expenses be paid out of my estate as soon after my death as is practicable.

SECOND: I may leave a statement or list giving certain items of my personal property to specific people. Any such statement or list in existence at my death shall be final.

THIRD: I give, devise, and bequeath all my estate, real, personal, and mixed, of whatever kind and wherever situated, of which I may die seized or possessed, or in which I may have any interest or over which I may have any power of appointment or testamentary disposition, to my spouse, _____. If my said spouse does not survive me, I give, and bequeath the said property to _____
_____
_____,
or the survivor of them.

FOURTH: In the event that any beneficiary fails to survive me by thirty days, then this will shall take effect as if that person had predeceased me.

FIFTH: I hereby nominate, constitute, and appoint _____ as Personal Representative of this, my Last Will and Testament. In the event that such named person is unable or unwilling to serve at any time or for any reason then I nominate, constitute, and appoint _____ as Personal Representative in the place and stead of the person first named herein. It is my will and I direct that my Personal Representative shall not be required to furnish a bond for the faithful performance of his or her duties in any jurisdiction, any provision of law to the contrary notwithstanding and I give my Personal Representative full power to administer my estate, including the power to settle claims, pay debts, and sell, lease or exchange real and personal property without court order..

IN WITNESS WHEREOF I declare this to be my Last Will and Testament and execute it willingly as my free and voluntary act for the purposes expressed herein and I am of legal age and sound mind and make this under no constraint or undue influence, this _____ day of _____, _____.

_____._____L.S.

The foregoing instrument was on said date subscribed at the end thereof by _____, the above named Testator who signed, published, and declared this instrument to be his/her Last Will and Testament in the presence of us and each of us, who thereupon at his/her request, in his/her presence, and in the presence of each other, have

Initials: _____ _____ _____ _____   Page ___ of ___
         Testator Witness   Witness   Witness

hereunto subscribed our names as witnesses thereto. We understand this to be his/her will and to the best of our knowledge testator is of legal age, of sound mind, and under no constraint or undue influence.

_____ residing at _____

_____ residing at _____

_____ residing at _____

Form 7. Simple Will—Spouse and no children

Last Will and Testament

I, _____ a resident of _____ County, North Carolina do hereby make, publish, and declare this to be my Last Will and Testament, hereby revoking any and all Wills and Codicils heretofore made by me.

FIRST: I direct that all my just debts and funeral expenses be paid out of my estate as soon after my death as is practicable.

SECOND: I may leave a statement or list giving certain items of my personal property to specific people. Any such statement or list in existence at my death shall be final.

THIRD: I give, devise, and bequeath all my estate, real, personal, and mixed, of whatever kind and wherever situated, of which I may die seized or possessed, or in which I may have any interest or over which I may have any power of appointment or testamentary disposition, to my spouse, _____. If my said spouse does not survive me, I give, and bequeath the said property to _____, or to their lineal descendants, per stirpes.

FOURTH: In the event that any beneficiary fails to survive me by thirty days, then this will shall take effect as if that person had predeceased me.

FIFTH: I hereby nominate, constitute, and appoint _____ as Personal Representative of this, my Last Will and Testament. In the event that such named person is unable or unwilling to serve at any time or for any reason then I nominate, constitute, and appoint _____ as Personal Representative in the place and stead of the person first named herein. It is my will and I direct that my Personal Representative shall not be required to furnish a bond for the faithful performance of his or her duties in any jurisdiction, any provision of law to the contrary notwithstanding and I give my Personal Representative full power to administer my estate, including the power to settle claims, pay debts, and sell, lease or exchange real and personal property without court order.

IN WITNESS WHEREOF I declare this to be my Last Will and Testament and execute it willingly as my free and voluntary act for the purposes expressed herein and I am of legal age and sound mind and make this under no constraint or undue influence, this _____ day of _____, _____.

_____L.S.

The foregoing instrument was on said date subscribed at the end thereof by _____, the above named Testator who signed, published, and declared this instrument to be his/her Last Will and Testament in the presence of us and each of us, who thereupon at his/her request, in his/her presence, and in the presence of each other, have

Initials: _____ _____ _____ _____ Page ____ of ____

Testator   Witness   Witness   Witness

hereunto subscribed our names as witnesses thereto. We understand this to be his/her will and to the best of our knowledge testator is of legal age, of sound mind, and under no constraint or undue influence.

_____ residing at _____

_____ residing at _____

_____ residing at _____

Form 8. Simple Will—Spouse and Adult children (all to spouse)

Last Will and Testament

I, _____ a resident of _____ County, North Carolina do hereby make, publish, and declare this to be my Last Will and Testament, hereby revoking any and all Wills and Codicils heretofore made by me.

FIRST: I direct that all my just debts and funeral expenses be paid out of my estate as soon after my death as is practicable.

SECOND: I may leave a statement or list giving certain items of my personal property to specific people. Any such statement or list in existence at my death shall be final.

THIRD: I give, devise, and bequeath all my estate, real, personal, and mixed, of whatever kind and wherever situated, of which I may die seized or possessed, or in which I may have any interest or over which I may have any power of appointment or testamentary disposition, to my spouse, _____. If my said spouse does not survive me, I give, and bequeath the said property to my children _____ _____ _____, in equal shares or to their lineal descendants, per stirpes.

FOURTH: In the event that any beneficiary fails to survive me by thirty days, then this will shall take effect as if that person had predeceased me.

FIFTH: I hereby nominate, constitute, and appoint _____ as Personal Representative of this, my Last Will and Testament. In the event that such named person is unable or unwilling to serve at any time or for any reason then I nominate, constitute, and appoint _____ as Personal Representative in the place and stead of the person first named herein. It is my will and I direct that my Personal Representative shall not be required to furnish a bond for the faithful performance of his or her duties in any jurisdiction, any provision of law to the contrary notwithstanding and I give my Personal Representative full power to administer my estate, including the power to settle claims, pay debts, and sell, lease or exchange real and personal property without court order.

IN WITNESS WHEREOF I declare this to be my Last Will and Testament and execute it willingly as my free and voluntary act for the purposes expressed herein and I am of legal age and sound mind and make this under no constraint or undue influence, this _____ day of _____, _____.

_____L.S.

The foregoing instrument was on said date subscribed at the end thereof by _____, the above named Testator who signed, published, and declared this instrument to be his/her Last Will and Testament in the presence of us and each of us, who thereupon at his/her request, in his/her presence, and in the presence of each other, have

Initials: _____ _____ _____ _____   Page ___ of ___
         Testator Witness Witness Witness

hereunto subscribed our names as witnesses thereto. We understand this to be his/her will and to the best of our knowledge testator is of legal age, of sound mind, and under no constraint or undue influence.

_____ residing at _____

_____ residing at _____

_____ residing at _____

Form 9. Simple Will—Spouse and Adult children (to spouse and children)

Last Will and Testament

I, _____ a resident of _____ County, North Carolina do hereby make, publish, and declare this to be my Last Will and Testament, hereby revoking any and all Wills and Codicils heretofore made by me.

FIRST: I direct that all my just debts and funeral expenses be paid out of my estate as soon after my death as is practicable.

SECOND: I may leave a statement or list giving certain items of my personal property to specific people. Any such statement or list in existence at my death shall be final.

THIRD: I give, devise, and bequeath all my estate, real, personal, and mixed, of whatever kind and wherever situated, of which I may die seized or possessed, or in which I may have any interest or over which I may have any power of appointment or testamentary disposition, as follows:
_____% to my spouse, _____ and
_____% to my children, _____
_____
_____ ,
in equal shares or to their lineal descendants per stirpes.

FOURTH: In the event that any beneficiary fails to survive me by thirty days, then this will shall take effect as if that person had predeceased me.

FIFTH: I hereby nominate, constitute, and appoint _____ as Personal Representative of this, my Last Will and Testament. In the event that such named person is unable or unwilling to serve at any time or for any reason then I nominate, constitute, and appoint _____ as Personal Representative in the place and stead of the person first named herein. It is my will and I direct that my Personal Representative shall not be required to furnish a bond for the faithful performance of his or her duties in any jurisdiction, any provision of law to the contrary notwithstanding and I give my Personal Representative full power to administer my estate, including the power to settle claims, pay debts, and sell, lease or exchange real and personal property without court order.

IN WITNESS WHEREOF I declare this to be my Last Will and Testament and execute it willingly as my free and voluntary act for the purposes expressed herein and I am of legal age and sound mind and make this under no constraint or undue influence, this _____ day of _____, _____.

_____L.S.

The foregoing instrument was on said date subscribed at the end thereof by _____, the above named Testator who signed, published, and declared this instrument to be his/her Last Will and Testament in the presence of us and each of us, who thereupon at his/her request, in his/her presence, and in the presence of each other, have

Initials: _____ _____ _____ _____   Page ____ of ____
         Testator Witness   Witness   Witness

hereunto subscribed our names as witnesses thereto. We understand this to be his/her will and to the best of our knowledge testator is of legal age, of sound mind, and under no constraint or undue influence.

_____residing at_____

_____residing at_____

_____residing at_____

Last Will and Testament

I, _____ a resident of _____ County, North Carolina do hereby make, publish, and declare this to be my Last Will and Testament, hereby revoking any and all Wills and Codicils heretofore made by me.

FIRST: I direct that all my just debts and funeral expenses be paid out of my estate as soon after my death as is practicable.

SECOND: I may leave a statement or list giving certain items of my personal property to specific people. Any such statement or list in existence at my death shall be final.

THIRD: I give, devise, and bequeath all my estate, real, personal, and mixed, of whatever kind and wherever situated, of which I may die seized or possessed, or in which I may have any interest or over which I may have any power of appointment or testamentary disposition, to my children _____, plus any afterborn or adopted children in equal shares or to their lineal descendants per stirpes.

FOURTH: In the event that any beneficiary fails to survive me by thirty days, then this will shall take effect as if that person had predeceased me.

FOURTH: In the event any of my children have not attained the age of 18 years at the time of my death, I hereby nominate, constitute, and appoint _____ as guardian over the person and estate of any of my children who have not reached the age of majority at the time of my death. In the event that said guardian is unable or unwilling to serve then I nominate, constitute, and appoint _____ as guardian. Said guardian to serve without bond or surety.

FIFTH: I hereby nominate, constitute, and appoint _____ as Personal Representative of this, my Last Will and Testament. In the event that such named person is unable or unwilling to serve at any time or for any reason then I nominate, constitute, and appoint _____ as Personal Representative in the place and stead of the person first named herein. It is my will and I direct that my Personal Representative shall not be required to furnish a bond for the faithful performance of his or her duties in any jurisdiction, any provision of law to the contrary notwithstanding and I give my Personal Representative full power to administer my estate, including the power to settle claims, pay debts, and sell, lease or exchange real and personal property without court order.

IN WITNESS WHEREOF I declare this to be my Last Will and Testament and execute it willingly as my free and voluntary act for the purposes expressed herein and I am of legal age and sound mind and make this under no constraint or undue influence, this _____ day of _____, _____.

Initials: _____ _____ _____ _____ Page ___ of ___
Testator   Witness   Witness   Witness

_____L.S.

    The foregoing instrument was on said date subscribed at the end thereof by _____, the above named Testator who signed, published, and declared this instrument to be his/her Last Will and Testament in the presence of us and each of us, who thereupon at his/her request, in his/her presence, and in the presence of each other, have hereunto subscribed our names as witnesses thereto. We understand this to be his/her will and to the best of our knowledge testator is of legal age, of sound mind, and under no constraint or undue influence.

_____residing at_____

_____residing at_____

_____residing at_____

Form 11. Simple Will—No Spouse—Minor Children—Two Guardians

Last Will and Testament

I, _____ a resident of _____ County, North Carolina do hereby make, publish, and declare this to be my Last Will and Testament, hereby revoking any and all Wills and Codicils heretofore made by me.

FIRST: I direct that all my just debts and funeral expenses be paid out of my estate as soon after my death as is practicable.

SECOND: I may leave a statement or list giving certain items of my personal property to specific people. Any such statement or list in existence at my death shall be final.

THIRD: I give, devise, and bequeath all my estate, real, personal, and mixed, of whatever kind and wherever situated, of which I may die seized or possessed, or in which I may have any interest or over which I may have any power of appointment or testamentary disposition, to my children _____, plus any afterborn or adopted children in equal shares or to their lineal descendants per stirpes.

FOURTH: In the event that any beneficiary fails to survive me by thirty days, then this will shall take effect as if that person had predeceased me.

FIFTH: In the event any of my children have not attained the age of 18 years at the time of my death, I hereby nominate, constitute, and appoint _____ as guardian over the person of any of my children who have not reached the age of majority at the time of my death. In the event that said guardian is unable or unwilling to serve then I nominate, constitute, and appoint _____ as guardian. Said guardian to serve without bond or surety.

SIXTH: In the event any of my children have not attained the age of 18 years at the time of my death, I hereby nominate, constitute, and appoint _____ as guardian over the property of any of my children who have not reached the age of majority at the time of my death. In the event that said guardian is unable or unwilling to serve then I nominate, constitute, and appoint _____ as guardian. Said guardian to serve without bond or surety.

SEVENTH: I hereby nominate, constitute, and appoint _____ as Personal Representative of this, my Last Will and Testament. In the event that such named person is unable or unwilling to serve at any time or for any reason then I nominate, constitute, and appoint _____ as Personal Representative in the place and stead of the person first named herein. It is my will and I direct that my Personal Representative shall not be required to furnish a bond for the faithful performance of his or her duties in any jurisdiction, any provision of law to the contrary notwithstanding and I give my Personal Representative full power

Initials: _____ _____ _____ _____   Page ____ of ____
        Testator   Witness   Witness   Witness

to administer my estate, including the power to settle claims, pay debts, and sell, lease or exchange real and personal property without court order.

IN WITNESS WHEREOF I declare this to be my Last Will and Testament and execute it willingly as my free and voluntary act for the purposes expressed herein and I am of legal age and sound mind and make this under no constraint or undue influence, this _____ day of _____, _____.

_____L.S.

The foregoing instrument was on said date subscribed at the end thereof by _____, the above named Testator who signed, published, and declared this instrument to be his/her Last Will and Testament in the presence of us and each of us, who thereupon at his/her request, in his/her presence, and in the presence of each other, have hereunto subscribed our names as witnesses thereto. We understand this to be his/her will and to the best of our knowledge testator is of legal age, of sound mind, and under no constraint or undue influence.

_____residing at_____

_____residing at_____

_____residing at_____

Form 12. Simple Will—No Spouse—Minor Children—Guardian and Trust

Last Will and Testament

I, _____ a resident of _____ County, North Carolina do hereby make, publish, and declare this to be my Last Will and Testament, hereby revoking any and all Wills and Codicils heretofore made by me.

FIRST: I direct that all my just debts and funeral expenses be paid out of my estate as soon after my death as is practicable.

SECOND: I may leave a statement or list giving certain items of my personal property to specific people. Any such statement or list in existence at my death shall be final.

THIRD: I give, devise, and bequeath all my estate, real, personal, and mixed, of whatever kind and wherever situated, of which I may die seized or possessed, or in which I may have any interest or over which I may have any power of appointment or testamentary disposition, to my children _____
_____
_____,
plus any afterborn or adopted children in equal shares or to their lineal descendants per stirpes.

FOURTH: In the event that any beneficiary fails to survive me by thirty days, then this will shall take effect as if that person had predeceased me.

FIFTH: In the event that any of my children have not reached the age of _____ years at the time of my death, then the share of any such child shall be held in a separate trust by _____ for such child.

The trustee shall use the income and that part of the principal of the trust as is, in the trustee's sole discretion, necessary or desirable to provide proper housing, medical care, food, clothing, entertainment and education for the trust beneficiary, considering the beneficiary's other resources. Any income that is not distributed shall be added to the principal. Additionally, the trustee shall have all powers conferred by the law of the state having jurisdiction over this trust, as well as the power to pay from the assets of the trust reasonable fees necessary to administer the trust.

The trust shall terminate when the child reaches the age specified above and the remaining assets distributed to the child, unless they have been exhausted sooner. In the event the child dies prior to the termination of the trust, then the assets shall pass to the estate of the child. The interests of the beneficiary under this trust shall not be assignable and shall be free from the claims of creditors to the full extent allowed by law.

In the event the said trustee is unable or unwilling to serve for any reason, then I nominate, constitute, and appoint _____ as alternate trustee. No bond shall be required of either trustee in any jurisdiction and this trust shall be administered without court supervision as allowed by law.

Initials: _____ _____ _____ _____   Page ____ of ____
        Testator   Witness   Witness   Witness

SIXTH: In the event any of my children have not attained the age of 18 years at the time of my death, I hereby nominate, constitute, and appoint _____ as guardian over the property of any of my children who have not reached the age of majority at the time of my death. In the event that said guardian is unable or unwilling to serve then I nominate, constitute, and appoint _____ as guardian. Said guardian to serve without bond or surety.

SEVENTH: I hereby nominate, constitute, and appoint _____ as Personal Representative of this, my Last Will and Testament. In the event that such named person is unable or unwilling to serve at any time or for any reason then I nominate, constitute, and appoint _____ as Personal Representative in the place and stead of the person first named herein. It is my will and I direct that my Personal Representative shall not be required to furnish a bond for the faithful performance of his or her duties in any jurisdiction, any provision of law to the contrary notwithstanding and I give my Personal Representative full power to administer my estate, including the power to settle claims, pay debts, and sell, lease or exchange real and personal property without court order.

IN WITNESS WHEREOF I declare this to be my Last Will and Testament and execute it willingly as my free and voluntary act for the purposes expressed herein and I am of legal age and sound mind and make this under no constraint or undue influence, this _____ day of _____, _____.

_____L.S.

The foregoing instrument was on said date subscribed at the end thereof by _____, the above named Testator who signed, published, and declared this instrument to be his/her Last Will and Testament in the presence of us and each of us, who thereupon at his/her request, in his/her presence, and in the presence of each other, have hereunto subscribed our names as witnesses thereto. We understand this to be his/her will and to the best of our knowledge testator is of legal age, of sound mind, and under no constraint or undue influence.

_____residing at_____

_____residing at_____

_____residing at_____

Form 13. Simple Will—No Spouse—Adult Children (equal by family)

Last Will and Testament

I, _____ a resident of _____ County, North Carolina do hereby make, publish, and declare this to be my Last Will and Testament, hereby revoking any and all Wills and Codicils heretofore made by me.

FIRST: I direct that all my just debts and funeral expenses be paid out of my estate as soon after my death as is practicable.

SECOND: I may leave a statement or list giving certain items of my personal property to specific people. Any such statement or list in existence at my death shall be final.

THIRD: I give, devise, and bequeath all my estate, real, personal, and mixed, of whatever kind and wherever situated, of which I may die seized or possessed, or in which I may have any interest or over which I may have any power of appointment or testamentary disposition, to my children _____
_____
_____,
in equal shares, or their lineal descendants per stirpes.

FOURTH: In the event that any beneficiary fails to survive me by thirty days, then this will shall take effect as if that person had predeceased me.

FIFTH: Should my spouse not survive me, I hereby nominate, constitute, and appoint _____ as guardian over the person and estate of any of my children who have not reached the age of majority at the time of my death. In the event that said guardian is unable or unwilling to serve then I nominate, constitute, and appoint _____ as guardian. Said guardian to serve without bond or surety.

SIXTH: I hereby nominate, constitute, and appoint _____ as Personal Representative of this, my Last Will and Testament. In the event that such named person is unable or unwilling to serve at any time or for any reason then I nominate, constitute, and appoint _____ as Personal Representative in the place and stead of the person first named herein. It is my will and I direct that my Personal Representative shall not be required to furnish a bond for the faithful performance of his or her duties in any jurisdiction, any provision of law to the contrary notwithstanding and I give my Personal Representative full power to administer my estate, including the power to settle claims, pay debts, and sell, lease or exchange real and personal property without court order.

IN WITNESS WHEREOF I declare this to be my Last Will and Testament and execute it willingly as my free and voluntary act for the purposes expressed herein and I am of legal age and sound mind and make this under no constraint or undue influence, this _____ day of _____, _____.

Initials: _____ _____ _____ _____ Page ____ of ____
            Testator   Witness   Witness   Witness

_____L.S.

The foregoing instrument was on said date subscribed at the end thereof by _____, the above named Testator who signed, published, and declared this instrument to be his/her Last Will and Testament in the presence of us and each of us, who thereupon at his/her request, in his/her presence, and in the presence of each other, have hereunto subscribed our names as witnesses thereto. We understand this to be his/her will and to the best of our knowledge testator is of legal age, of sound mind, and under no constraint or undue influence.

_____residing at_____

_____residing at_____

_____residing at_____

Form 14. Simple Will—No Spouse—Adult Children (equal by person)

Last Will and Testament

I, _____ a resident of _____ County, North Carolina do hereby make, publish, and declare this to be my Last Will and Testament, hereby revoking any and all Wills and Codicils heretofore made by me.

FIRST: I direct that all my just debts and funeral expenses be paid out of my estate as soon after my death as is practicable.

SECOND: I may leave a statement or list giving certain items of my personal property to specific people. Any such statement or list in existence at my death shall be final.

THIRD: I give, devise, and bequeath all my estate, real, personal, and mixed, of whatever kind and wherever situated, of which I may die seized or possessed, or in which I may have any interest or over which I may have any power of appointment or testamentary disposition, to my children _____
_____
_____,
in equal shares, or their lineal descendants per capita.

FOURTH: In the event that any beneficiary fails to survive me by thirty days, then this will shall take effect as if that person had predeceased me.

FIFTH: Should my spouse not survive me, I hereby nominate, constitute, and appoint _____ as guardian over the person and estate of any of my children who have not reached the age of majority at the time of my death. In the event that said guardian is unable or unwilling to serve then I nominate, constitute, and appoint _____ as guardian. Said guardian shall serve without bond or surety.

SIXTH: I hereby nominate, constitute, and appoint _____ as Personal Representative of this, my Last Will and Testament. In the event that such named person is unable or unwilling to serve at any time or for any reason then I nominate, constitute, and appoint _____ as Personal Representative in the place and stead of the person first named herein. It is my will and I direct that my Personal Representative shall not be required to furnish a bond for the faithful performance of his or her duties in any jurisdiction, any provision of law to the contrary notwithstanding and I give my Personal Representative full power to administer my estate, including the power to settle claims, pay debts, and sell, lease or exchange real and personal property without court order.

IN WITNESS WHEREOF I declare this to be my Last Will and Testament and execute it willingly as my free and voluntary act for the purposes expressed herein and I am of legal age and sound mind and make this under no constraint or undue influence, this _____ day of _____, _____.

Initials: _____ _____ _____ _____   Page ___ of ___
           Testator   Witness   Witness   Witness

_____L.S.

    The foregoing instrument was on said date subscribed at the end thereof by _____, the above named Testator who signed, published, and declared this instrument to be his/her Last Will and Testament in the presence of us and each of us, who thereupon at his/her request, in his/her presence, and in the presence of each other, have hereunto subscribed our names as witnesses thereto. We understand this to be his/her will and to the best of our knowledge testator is of legal age, of sound mind, and under no constraint or undue influence.

_____residing at_____

_____residing at_____

_____residing at_____

Form 15. Simple Will—No spouse and no children (to survivor)

Last Will and Testament

I, _____ a resident of _____ County, North Carolina do hereby make, publish, and declare this to be my Last Will and Testament, hereby revoking any and all Wills and Codicils heretofore made by me.

FIRST: I direct that all my just debts and funeral expenses be paid out of my estate as soon after my death as is practicable.

SECOND: I may leave a statement or list giving certain items of my personal property to specific people. Any such statement or list in existence at my death shall be final.

THIRD: I give, devise, and bequeath all my estate, real, personal, and mixed, of whatever kind and wherever situated, of which I may die seized or possessed, or in which I may have any interest or over which I may have any power of appointment or testamentary disposition, to the following:_____
_____
_____, or to the survivor of them.

FOURTH: In the event that any beneficiary fails to survive me by thirty days, then this will shall take effect as if that person had predeceased me.

FIFTH: I hereby nominate, constitute, and appoint _____ as Personal Representative of this, my Last Will and Testament. In the event that such named person is unable or unwilling to serve at any time or for any reason then I nominate, constitute, and appoint _____ as Personal Representative in the place and stead of the person first named herein. It is my will and I direct that my Personal Representative shall not be required to furnish a bond for the faithful performance of his or her duties in any jurisdiction, any provision of law to the contrary notwithstanding and I give my Personal Representative full power to administer my estate, including the power to settle claims, pay debts, and sell, lease or exchange real and personal property without court order.

IN WITNESS WHEREOF I declare this to be my Last Will and Testament and execute it willingly as my free and voluntary act for the purposes expressed herein and I am of legal age and sound mind and make this under no constraint or undue influence, this _____ day of _____, _____.

_____L.S.

The foregoing instrument was on said date subscribed at the end thereof by _____, the above named Testator who signed, published, and declared this instrument to be his/her Last Will and Testament in the presence of us and each of us, who thereupon at his/her request, in his/her presence, and in the presence of each other, have hereunto subscribed our names as witnesses thereto. We understand this to be his/her will and to the

Initials: _____ _____ _____ _____   Page ____ of ____

| Testator | Witness | Witness | Witness |

best of our knowledge testator is of legal age, of sound mind, and under no constraint or undue influence.

_____residing at_____

_____residing at_____

_____residing at_____

Form 16. Simple Will—No spouse and no children (to children and grandchildren)

Last Will and Testament

I, _____ a resident of _____ County, North Carolina do hereby make, publish, and declare this to be my Last Will and Testament, hereby revoking any and all Wills and Codicils heretofore made by me.

FIRST: I direct that all my just debts and funeral expenses be paid out of my estate as soon after my death as is practicable.

SECOND: I may leave a statement or list giving certain items of my personal property to specific people. Any such statement or list in existence at my death shall be final.

THIRD: I give, devise, and bequeath all my estate, real, personal, and mixed, of whatever kind and wherever situated, of which I may die seized or possessed, or in which I may have any interest or over which I may have any power of appointment or testamentary disposition, to the following _____
_____
_____,
in equal shares, or their lineal descendants per stirpes.

FOURTH: In the event that any beneficiary fails to survive me by thirty days, then this will shall take effect as if that person had predeceased me.

FIFTH: I hereby nominate, constitute, and appoint _____ as Personal Representative of this, my Last Will and Testament. In the event that such named person is unable or unwilling to serve at any time or for any reason then I nominate, constitute, and appoint _____ as Personal Representative in the place and stead of the person first named herein. It is my will and I direct that my Personal Representative shall not be required to furnish a bond for the faithful performance of his or her duties in any jurisdiction, any provision of law to the contrary notwithstanding and I give my Personal Representative full power to administer my estate, including the power to settle claims, pay debts, and sell, lease or exchange real and personal property without court order.

IN WITNESS WHEREOF I declare this to be my Last Will and Testament and execute it willingly as my free and voluntary act for the purposes expressed herein and I am of legal age and sound mind and make this under no constraint or undue influence, this _____ day of _____, _____.

_____L.S.

The foregoing instrument was on said date subscribed at the end thereof by _____, the above named Testator who signed, published, and declared this instrument to be his/her Last Will and Testament in the presence of us and each of us, who thereupon at his/her request, in his/her presence, and in the presence of each other, have hereunto subscribed our names as witnesses thereto. We understand this to be his/her will and to the

Initials: _____ _____ _____ _____   Page ____ of ____

Testator   Witness   Witness   Witness

best of our knowledge testator is of legal age, of sound mind, and under no constraint or undue influence.

_____residing at_____

_____residing at_____

_____residing at_____

Form 17. Self-proved will affidavit

Self-Proved Will Affidavit
(attach to Will)

STATE OF NORTH CAROLINA

COUNTY OF _____

    I, the undersigned, an officer authorized to administer oaths, certify that _____, the testator and _____, _____, and _____, the witnesses, whose names are signed to the attached or foregoing instrument and whose signatures appear below, having appeared before me and having been first been duly sworn, each then declared to me that: 1) the attached or foregoing instrument is the last will of the testator; 2) the testator willingly and voluntarily declared, signed and executed the will in the presence of the witnesses; 3) the witnesses signed the will upon the request of the testator, in the presence and hearing of the testator and in the presence of each other; 4) to the best knowledge of each witness, the testator was, at the time of signing, of the age of majority (or otherwise legally competent to make a will), of sound mind and memory and under no constraint or undue influence; and 5) each witness was and is competent and of proper age to witness a will.

                                                                                  _____ (Testator)

                                                                                  _____ (Witness)

                                                                                  _____ (Witness)

                                                                                  _____ (Witness)

Subscribed, sworn and acknowledged before me by _____, the testator, and by _____ , _____, _____, witnesses, this _____ day of _____, _____.

_____
Notary or other officer

Initials: _____ _____ _____ _____   Page ____ of ____
        Testator   Witness   Witness   Witness

Form 18. Codicil to Will

First Codicil to the Will of

_____

I, _____, a resident of _____ County, North Carolina declare this to be the first codicil to my Last Will and Testament dated _____, _____.

FIRST: I hereby revoke the clause of my Will which reads as follows:
_____
_____
_____
_____

SECOND: I hereby add following clause to my Will: _____
_____
_____
_____
_____.

THIRD: In all other respects I hereby confirm and republish my Last Will and Testament dated _____, _____.

IN WITNESS WHEREOF, I have signed, published and declared the foregoing instrument as and for a codicil to my Last Will and Testament, this _____ day of _____, _____.

_____

The foregoing instrument was on the _____ day of _____, _____, signed at the end thereof, and at the same time published and declared by _____, as and for a codicil to his/her Last Will and Testament, dated _____, _____, in the presence of each of us, who, this attestation clause having been read to us, did at the request of the said testator/testatrix, in his/her presence and in the presence of each other signed our names as witnesses thereto.

_____ residing at _____

_____ residing at _____

Initials: _____ _____ _____ _____   Page ____ of ____

Testator   Witness   Witness   Witness

Self-Proved Codicil Affidavit
(attach to Codicil)

STATE OF NORTH CAROLINA

COUNTY OF _____

    I, the undersigned, an officer authorized to administer oaths, certify that _____, the testator and _____, _____ and _____, the witnesses, whose names are signed to the attached or foregoing instrument and whose signatures appear below, having appeared before me and having been first been duly sworn, each then declared to me that: 1) the attached or foregoing instrument is a codicil to the last will of the testator; 2) the testator willingly and voluntarily declared, signed and executed the codicil in the presence of the witnesses; 3) the witnesses signed the codicil upon the request of the testator, in the presence and hearing of the testator and in the presence of each other; 4) to the best knowledge of each witness, the testator was, at the time of signing, of the age of majority (or otherwise legally competent to make a will), of sound mind, and memory and under no constraint or undue influence; and 5) each witness was and is competent and of proper age to witness a codicil to a will.

_____ (Testator)

_____ (Witness)

_____ (Witness)

_____ (Witness)

Subscribed, sworn and acknowledged before me by _____, the testator, and by _____, _____, and _____, witnesses, this _____ day of _____.

_____
Notary or other officer

DECLARATION OF A DESIRE FOR NATURAL DEATH

I, _____, being of sound mind,, desire that, as specified below, my life not be prolonged by extraordinary means or by artificial nutrition or hydration if my condition is determined to be terminal and incurable or if I am diagnosed as being in a persistent vegetative state. I am aware and understand that this writing authorizes a physician to withhold or discontinue extraordinary means or artificial nutrition or hydration, in accordance with my specifications set forth below:

(Initial any of the following, as desired:)

_____ If my condition is determined to be terminal and incurable, I authorize the following:

    _____ My physician may withhold or discontinue extraordinary means only.

    _____ In addition to withholding or discontinuing extraordinary means if such are necessary, my physician may withhold or discontinue either artificial nutrition or hydration, or both.

_____ If my physician determines that I am in a persistent vegetative state, I authorize the following:

    _____ My physician may withhold or discontinue extraordinary means only.

    _____ In addition to withholding or discontinuing extraordinary means if such are necessary, my physician may withhold or discontinue either artificial nutrition or hydration, or both.

This the _____ day of _____, _____.

_____
Declarant

I hereby state that the Declarant, _____, being of sound mind, signed the above declaration in my presence and that I am not related to the Declarant by blood or marriage and that I do not now or have a reasonable expectation that I would be entitled to any portion of the estate of the Declarant under any existing Will or Codicil of the Declarant, or as an heir under the Intestate Succession Act if the Declarant died on this date without a will. I also state that I am not the Declarant's attending physician, or an employee of the Declarant's attending physician, or an employee of a health facility in which the Declarant is a patient, or an employee of a Nursing Home or any group care home, where the Declarant resides. I further state that I do not now have any claim against the Declarant.

_____
Witness

_____
Witness

NORTH CAROLINA
COUNTY OF _____

CERTIFICATE

I, a Notary Public in and for the State of North Carolina, hereby certify that _____, the Declarant, appeared before me and swore to me and to the witnesses in my presence that this instrument is his/her Declaration of a Desire For a Natural Death, and that he/she had willingly and voluntarily made and executed it as his/her free act and deed for the purposes expressed in it.

I further certify that _____ and _____, witnesses, appeared before me and swore that they witnessed _____, the declarant, sign the attached declaration, believing him/her to be of sound mind; and also swore that at the time they witnessed the declaration (i) they were not related within the third degree to the Declarant or to any Declarant's spouse, and (ii) that they did not now or have a reasonable expectation that they would be entitled to any portion of the Estate of the Declarant upon the Declarant's death under any Will of the Declarant, or Codicil thereto, then existing or under the Intestate Succession Act as it provides at that time, (iii) they were not a physician attending the Declarant, or any employee of an attending physician, or an employee of a health facility in which the Declarant was a patient, or of a nursing home or of any group care home, in which the Declarant resided, and (iv) they did not have a claim against the Declarant. I further certify that I am satisfied as to the genuineness and due execution of the Declaration.

This the _____ day of _____, _____.

_____
Notary Public

(NOTARY SEAL)

Instrument of Anatomical Gift

I, _____, of _____, North Carolina, make this anatomical gift to take effect upon my death and prior to embalmment of my body, revoking all prior anatomical gift instruments made by me.

FIRST: I give the North Carolina EYE BANK of Raleigh, North Carolina, or to any eye bank serving the area in which my death occurs, both or either of my eyes for such use as the Donee may see fit with regard to all or any part of said eyes.

SECOND: I give any organ of my body (other than my eyes) to be used for any appropriate purpose and authorize any portion of my body to be transplanted to the body of any other person.

THIRD: I give my entire body to _____ Medical School, for the promotion of anatomical study and teaching or any medical school in the area in which my death occurs. I direct that after these purposes have been accomplished, (my remains OR the remainder of my body be cremated and remains) be buried in _____ Cemetery with the services of the (Priest) (Minister) (Rabbi) of the _____ faith.

WITNESS, I the Donor, have signed this _____ day of _____, _____.

_____
(DONOR)

This instrument was signed by _____, in our presence, and in the presence of each other as witnesses, this _____ day of _____, _____.

_____ residing at _____
Witness

_____ residing at _____
Witness

_____ residing at _____
Witness

Form 22. Organ Donor Card

UNIFORM DONOR CARD

The undersigned hereby makes this anatomical gift, if medically acceptable, to take effect on death. The words and marks below indicate my desires:

I give:

    (a) ____ any needed organs or parts;

    (b) ____ only the following organs or parts

_____

for the purpose of transplantation, therapy, medical research, or education;

    (c) ____ my body for anatomical study if needed.

Limitations or special wishes, if any:

_____

Signed by the donor and the following witnesses in the presence of each other:

Signature of Donor	Date of birth
Date signed	City & State
Witness	Witness
Address	Address

UNIFORM DONOR CARD

The undersigned hereby makes this anatomical gift, if medically acceptable, to take effect on death. The words and marks below indicate my desires:

I give:

    (a) ____ any needed organs or parts;

    (b) ____ only the following organs or parts

_____

for the purpose of transplantation, therapy, medical research, or education;

    (c) ____ my body for anatomical study if needed.

Limitations or special wishes, if any:

_____

Signed by the donor and the following witnesses in the presence of each other:

Signature of Donor	Date of birth
Date signed	City & State
Witness	Witness
Address	Address

UNIFORM DONOR CARD

The undersigned hereby makes this anatomical gift, if medically acceptable, to take effect on death. The words and marks below indicate my desires:

I give:

    (a) ____ any needed organs or parts;

    (b) ____ only the following organs or parts

_____

for the purpose of transplantation, therapy, medical research, or education;

    (c) ____ my body for anatomical study if needed.

Limitations or special wishes, if any:

_____

Signed by the donor and the following witnesses in the presence of each other:

Signature of Donor	Date of birth
Date signed	City & State
Witness	Witness
Address	Address

UNIFORM DONOR CARD

The undersigned hereby makes this anatomical gift, if medically acceptable, to take effect on death. The words and marks below indicate my desires:

I give:

    (a) ____ any needed organs or parts;

    (b) ____ only the following organs or parts

_____

for the purpose of transplantation, therapy, medical research, or education;

    (c) ____ my body for anatomical study if needed.

Limitations or special wishes, if any:

_____

Signed by the donor and the following witnesses in the presence of each other:

Signature of Donor	Date of birth
Date signed	City & State
Witness	Witness
Address	Address

One of these cards should be cut out and carried in your wallet or purse.

Index

A

administrator, 15
alternate beneficiaries, 28
anatomical gifts, 43
avoiding probate, 5

B

beneficiaries, 19
beneficiary, 15
bequest, 15
blind testators, 24

C

changing a will, 38
children's trust, 31
children, 5, 13, 25, 31
codicil, 16, 38, 97
complicated estates, 24
conditions on gifts, 23, 24

D

debts, 14
decedent, 16
descendant, 16
devise, 16
disinheriting someone, 33
divorce, 14

E

elective share, 16
executing a will, 35

executor, 16
exempt property, 12, 16

F

family allowance, 12, 16
family, 29
forced share, 9, 10, 16
forms, 34, 57
funeral arrangements, 34

G

guardian, 5, 19, 30

H

handwritten will, 22
heir, 16
holographic will, 22

I

I/T/F accounts, 11
illegal conditions, 23
instrument of anatomical gift, 103
intestate share, 16
intestate, 16, 20

J

joint beneficiaries, 27
joint tenancy, 6, 7, 8
joint tenancy, 16

L

legacy, 16
living trusts, 5
living will, 17, 41, 101

M

marriage, 13

N

notary, 36, 41

O

oral will, 23
organizations, 25
out-of-state will, 21

P

parties, 25
people named in will, 25
per capita, 29
per stirpes, 29
personal property
personal representative, 14, 17, 19, 32
POD accounts, 11
probate, 5, 17

R

real estate, 26
remainder clause, 28
residue, 17

reviving a will, 38
revoking a will, 38

S

safe deposit box, 37
sample filled-in forms, 45
secured debts, 14
self-proved will, 20, 33
specific bequest, 17, 26
spouse, 9, 25
storing a will, 37
survivorship, 30

T

tangible property, 26
taxes, 20, 27
tenancy by the entireties, 8, 17
tenancy in common, 8, 17
testate, 17
testator, 17
TOD accounts, 11
trusts, 5, 31

U

uniform donor card, 43, 105
usual dwelling place, 11

W

will contest, 24
witnessed will, 22
witnesses, 32, 35

Your #1 Source for Real World Legal Information...

LEGAL SURVIVAL GUIDES™

- Written by lawyers
- Simple English explanation of the law
- Forms and instructions included

 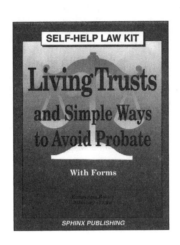 

THE POWER OF ATTORNEY HANDBOOK (2ND EDITION)

It is now easier than ever to authorize someone to act on your behalf for your convenience or necessity. Forms with instructions are included, as well as a state-by-state reference guide to power of attorney laws.

140 pages; $19.95;
ISBN 1-57248-044-0

LIVING TRUSTS AND SIMPLE WAYS TO AVOID PROBATE

What everyone needs to know about probate and who needs to avoid it. Included are forms for creating your own living trust without a lawyer. Even if you don't use a trust, this book can save hundreds of dollars in lawyer and probate fees.

140 pages; $19.95;
ISBN 1-57248-019-X

LEGAL RESEARCH MADE EASY

This book for non-lawyers explains how to use the various types of legal reference books such as legal encyclopedias, statutes, digests, American Law Reports, and Shepard's Citations, as well as computerized legal databases. Includes state and federal materials.

124 pages; $14.95;
ISBN 1-57248-008-4

What our customers say about our books:

"It couldn't be more clear for the lay person." —R.D.

"I want you to know I really appreciate your book. It has saved me a lot of time and money." —L.T.

"Your real estate contracts book has saved me nearly $12,000.00 in closing costs over the past year." —A.B.

"...many of the legal questions that I have had over the years were answered clearly and concisely through your plain English interpretation of the law." —C.E.H.

"If there weren't people out there like you I'd be lost. You have the best books of this type out there." —S.B.

"...your forms and directions are easy to follow." —C.V.M.

Legal Survival Guides are directly available from the publisher, or from your local bookstores. For credit card orders call 1–800–43–BRIGHT, write P.O. Box 372, Naperville, IL 60566, or fax 630-961-2168

LEGAL SURVIVAL GUIDES™ NATIONAL TITLES
Valid in All 50 States

LEGAL SURVIVAL IN BUSINESS

How to Form Your Own Corporation (2E)	$19.95
How to Register Your Own Copyright (2E)	$19.95
How to Register Your Own Trademark (2E)	$19.95
Most Valuable Business Forms You'll Ever Need	$19.95
Most Valuable Corporate Forms You'll Ever Need	$24.95
Software Law (with diskette)	$29.95

LEGAL SURVIVAL IN COURT

Crime Victim's Guide to Justice	$19.95
Debtors' Rights (2E)	$12.95
Defend Yourself Against Criminal Charges	$19.95
Grandparents' Rights	$19.95
Help Your Lawyer Win Your Case	$12.95
Jurors' Rights	$9.95
Legal Malpractice and Other Claims Against Your Lawyer	$18.95
Legal Research Made Easy	$14.95
Simple Ways to Protect Yourself From Lawsuits	$24.95
Victim's Rights	$12.95
Winning Your Personal Injury Claim	$19.95

LEGAL SURVIVAL IN REAL ESTATE

How to Buy a Condominium or Townhome	$16.95
How to Negotiate Real Estate Contracts (2E)	$16.95
How to Negotiate Real Estate Leases (2E)	$16.95
Successful Real Estate Brokerage Management	$19.95

LEGAL SURVIVAL IN PERSONAL AFFAIRS

How to File Your Own Bankruptcy (4E)	$19.95
How to File Your Own Divorce (3E)	$19.95
How to Make Your Own Will	$12.95
How to Write Your Own Living Will	$9.95
Living Trusts and Simple Ways to Avoid Probate	$19.95
Neighbor vs. Neighbor	$12.95
Power of Attorney Handbook (2E)	$19.95
Social Security Benefits Handbook	$14.95
U.S.A. Immigration Guide (2E)	$19.95
Guia de Inmigracion a Estados Unidos	$19.95

Legal Survival Guides are directly available from the publisher, or from your local bookstores.

For credit card orders call 1–800–43–BRIGHT, write P.O. Box 372, Naperville, IL 60566, or fax 630-961-2168

LEGAL SURVIVAL GUIDES™ STATE TITLES
Up-to-date for Your State

NEW YORK

How to File for Divorce in NY	$19.95
How to Make a NY Will	$12.95
How to Start a Business in NY	$16.95
How to Win in Small Claims Court in NY	$14.95
Landlord's Rights and Duties in NY	$19.95
New York Power of Attorney Handbook	$12.95

PENNSYLVANIA

How to File for Divorce in PA	$19.95
How to Make a PA Will	$12.95
How to Start a Business in PA	$16.95
Landlord's Rights and Duties in PA	$19.95

FLORIDA

Florida Power of Attorney Handbook	$9.95
How to Change Your Name in FL (3E)	$14.95
How to File a FL Construction Lien (2E)	$19.95
How to File a Guardianship in FL	$19.95
How to File for Divorce in FL (4E)	$21.95
How to Form a Nonprofit Corp in FL (3E)	$19.95
How to Form a Simple Corp in FL (3E)	$19.95
How to Make a FL Will (4E)	$9.95
How to Modify Your FL Divorce Judgement (3E)	$22.95
How to Probate an Estate in FL (2E)	$24.95
How to Start a Business in FL (4E)	$16.95
How to Win in Small Claims Court in FL (5E)	$14.95
Land Trusts in FL (4E)	$24.95
Landlord's Rights and Duties in FL (6E)	$19.95
Women's Legal Rights in FL	$19.95

GEORGIA

How to File for Divorce in GA (2E)	$19.95
How to Make a GA Will (2E)	$9.95
How to Start and Run a GA Business (2E)	$18.95

ILLINOIS

How to File for Divorce in IL	$19.95
How to Make an IL Will	$9.95
How to Start a Business in IL	$16.95

MASSACHUSETTS

How to File for Divorce in MA	$19.95
How to Make a MA Will	$9.95
How to Probate an Estate in MA	$19.95
How to Start a Business in MA	$16.95
Landlord's Rights and Duties in MA	$19.95

MICHIGAN

How to File for Divorce in MI	$19.95
How to Make a MI Will	$9.95
How to Start a Business in MI	$16.95

MINNESOTA

How to File for Divorce in MN	$19.95
How to Form a Simple Corporation in MN	$19.95
How to Make a MN Will	$9.95
How to Start a Business in MN	$16.95

NORTH CAROLINA

How to File for Divorce in NC	$19.95
How to Make a NC Will	$9.95
How to Start a Business in NC	$16.95

TEXAS

How to File for Divorce in TX	$19.95
How to Form a Simple Corporation in TX	$19.95
How to Make a TX Will	$9.95
How to Probate an Estate in TX	$19.95
How to Start a Business in TX	$16.95
How to Win in Small Claims Court in TX	$14.95
Landlord's Rights and Duties in TX	$19.95

Legal Survival Guides are directly available from the publisher, or from your local bookstores. For credit card orders call 1–800–43–BRIGHT, write P.O. Box 372, Naperville, IL 60566, or fax 630-961-2168

Legal Survival Guides™ • Order Form

BILL TO:

SHIP TO:

| Phone # | Terms | F.O.B. Chicago, IL | Ship Date |

Charge my: ☐ VISA ☐ Mastercard ☐ American Express

☐ **Money Order** (no personal checks please)

Credit Card Number

Expiration Date

Qty	ISBN	Title	Retail
	Legal Survival Guides Fall 97 National Frontlist		
	1-57071-223-9	How to File Your Own Bankruptcy (4E)	$19.95
	1-57071-224-7	How to File Your Own Divorce (3E)	$19.95
	1-57071-227-1	How to Form Your Own Corporation (2E)	$19.95
	1-57071-228-X	How to Make Your Own Will	$12.95
	1-57071-225-5	How to Register Your Own Copyright (2E)	$19.95
	1-57071-226-3	How to Register Your Own Trademark (2E)	$19.95
	Fall 97 New York Frontlist		
	1-57071-184-4	How to File for Divorce in NY	$19.95
	1-57071-183-6	How to Make a NY Will	$12.95
	1-57071-185-2	How to Start a Business in NY	$16.95
	1-57071-187-9	How to Win in Small Claims Court in NY	$14.95
	1-57071-186-0	Landlord's Rights and Duties in NY	$19.95
	1-57071-188-7	New York Power of Attorney Handbook	$12.95
	Fall 97 Pennsylvania Frontlist		
	1-57071-177-1	How to File for Divorce in PA	$19.95
	1-57071-176-3	How to Make a PA Will	$12.95
	1-57071-178-X	How to Start a Business in PA	$16.95
	1-57071-179-8	Landlord's Rights and Duties in PA	$19.95
	Legal Survival Guides National Backlist		
	1-57071-166-6	Crime Victim's Guide to Justice	$19.95
	1-57248-023-8	Debtors' Rights (2E)	$12.95
	1-57071-162-3	Defend Yourself Against Criminal Charges	$19.95
	1-57248-001-7	Grandparents' Rights	$19.95
	0-913825-99-9	Guia de Inmigracion a Estados Unidos	$19.95
	1-57248-021-1	Help Your Lawyer Win Your Case	$12.95
	1-57071-164-X	How to Buy a Condominium or Townhome	$16.95
	1-57248-035-1	How to Negotiate Real Estate Contracts (2E)	$16.95
	1-57248-036-X	How to Negotiate Real Estate Leases (2E)	$16.95
	1-57071-167-4	How to Write Your Own Living Will	$9.95
	1-57248-031-9	Jurors' Rights	$9.95
	1-57248-032-7	Legal Malpractice and Other Claims Against Your Lawyer	$18.95
	1-57248-008-4	Legal Research Made Easy	$14.95
	1-57248-019-X	Living Trusts and Simple Ways to Avoid Probate	$19.95
	1-57248-022-X	Most Valuable Business Forms You'll Ever Need	$19.95
	1-57248-007-6	Most Valuable Corporate Forms You'll Ever Need	$24.95
	0-913825-41-7	Neighbor vs. Neighbor	$12.95
	1-57248-044-0	Power of Attorney Handbook (2E)	$19.95
	1-57248-020-3	Simple Ways to Protect Yourself From Lawsuits	$24.95
	1-57248-033-5	Social Security Benefits Handbook	$14.95
	1-57071-163-1	Software Law (w/diskette)	$29.95
	0-913825-86-7	Successful Real Estate Brokerage Mgmt.	$19.95
	1-57248-000-9	U.S.A. Immigration Guide (2E)	$19.95
	0-913825-82-4	Victim's Rights	$12.95
	1-57071-165-8	Winning Your Personal Injury Claim	$19.95
	Florida Backlist		
	0-913825-81-6	Florida Power of Attorney Handbook	$9.95
	1-57248-028-9	How to Change Your Name in FL (3E)	$14.95
	0-913825-84-0	How to File a FL Construction Lien (2E)	$19.95
	0-913825-53-0	How to File a Guardianship in FL	$19.95
	1-57248-046-7	How to File for Divorce in FL (4E)	$21.95

Qty	ISBN	Title	Retail
	Florida Backlist (cont')		
	1-57248-004-1	How to Form a Nonprofit Corp in FL (3E)	$19.95
	0-913825-96-4	How to Form a Simple Corp in FL (3E)	$19.95
	1-57248-027-0	How to Make a FL Will (4E)	$9.95
	1-57248-056-4	How to Modify Your FL Divorce Judgement (3E)	$22.95
	1-57248-003-3	How to Probate an Estate in FL (2E)	$24.95
	1-57248-005-X	How to Start a Business in FL (4E)	$16.95
	0-913825-97-2	How to Win in Small Claims Court in FL (5E)	$14.95
	1-57248-029-7	Land Trusts in FL (4E)	$24.95
	1-57248-057-2	Landlord's Rights and Duties in FL (6E)	$19.95
	0-913825-73-5	Women's Legal Rights in FL	$19.95
	Georgia Backlist		
	1-57248-058-0	How to File for Divorce in GA (2E)	$19.95
	1-57248-047-5	How to Make a GA Will (2E)	$9.95
	1-57248-026-2	How to Start and Run a GA Business (2E)	$18.95
	Illinois Backlist		
	1-57248-042-4	How to File for Divorce in IL	$19.95
	1-57248-043-2	How to Make an IL Will	$9.95
	1-57248-041-6	How to Start a Business in IL	$16.95
	Massachusetts Backlist		
	1-57248-051-3	How to File for Divorce in MA	$19.95
	1-57248-050-5	How to Make a MA Will	$9.95
	1-57248-053-X	How to Probate an Estate in MA	$19.95
	1-57248-054-8	How to Start a Business in MA	$16.95
	1-57248-055-6	Landlord's Rights and Duties in MA	$19.95
	Michigan Backlist		
	1-57248-014-9	How to File for Divorce in MI	$19.95
	1-57248-015-7	How to Make a MI Will	$9.95
	1-57248-013-0	How to Start a Business in MI	$16.95
	Minnesota Backlist		
	1-57248-039-4	How to File for Divorce in MN	$19.95
	1-57248-040-8	How to Form a Simple Corporation in MN	$19.95
	1-57248-037-8	How to Make a MN Will	$9.95
	1-57248-038-6	How to Start a Business in MN	$16.95
	North Carolina Backlist		
	0-913825-94-8	How to File for Divorce in NC	$19.95
	0-913825-92-1	How to Make a NC Will	$9.95
	0-913825-93-X	How to Start a Business in NC	$16.95
	Texas Backlist		
	0-913825-91-3	How to File for Divorce in TX	$19.95
	1-57248-009-2	How to Form a Simple Corporation in TX	$19.95
	0-913825-89-1	How to Make a TX Will	$9.95
	1-57248-010-6	How to Probate an Estate in TX	$19.95
	0-913825-90-5	How to Start a Business in TX	$16.95
	1-57248-012-2	How to Win in Small Claims Court in TX	$14.95
	1-57248-011-4	Landlord's Rights and Duties in TX	$19.95

SUBTOTAL

IL Residents add 6.75%, FL Residents add county sales tax

Shipping— $4.00 for 1st book, $1.00 each additional

Total

To order, call Sourcebooks at 1-800-43-BRIGHT or FAX (630)961-2168 (Bookstores, libraries, wholesalers—please call for discount)